YEARBOOK 2014

AUTOCAR

THE WORLD'S BEST CARS, BY THE WORLD'S BEST CAR WRITERS

Another year to remember

THE PAGES THAT follow feature, among many other vehicles, two of the greatest hyper cars ever made, a cutting-edge eco-mobile that is capable of covering more than 300 miles on a gallon of fuel, the most keenly anticipated new British sports car of the year and a monstrous six-wheeled leviathan that proves major car manufacturers *do* have a sense of humour.

Yes, it is fair to say the past year has been jam-packed with highlights on many fronts. Car makers have finally come to terms with the fact that driving enthusiasts now demand vehicles that are dramatic to look at, rewarding to drive, bristling with technology and extremely frugal to boot. As one key industry figure put it to me, "Nobody is interested in driving around in a grey box any more".

We've ensured this annual is completely free from bland cars. It draws together some of the most impressive vehicles we've driven during the past 12 months, recalls our stand-out road trip memories, and delves into the Autocar archives to unearth some of the interesting motors from decades past.

We hope you enjoy our celebration of the car.

MATT BURT
Yearbook editor

132
Family hatchbacks from Audi, Volvo, Ford and VW go head-to-head

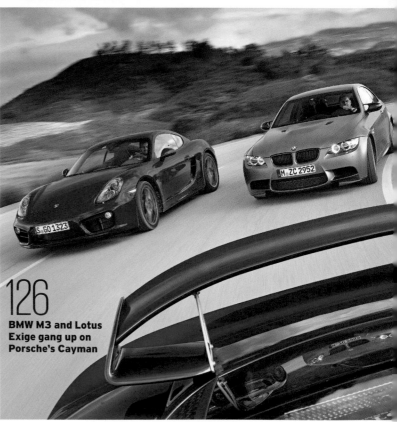

126
BMW M3 and Lotus Exige gang up on Porsche's Cayman

CONTENTS

FEATURES

BEST NEW CARS

SPORT

GREAT DRIVES

BUYING USED

94 Good, bad and ugly ideas from motor racing

102 Seven iterations of the Porsche 911 driven

Great cars go head-to-head in Autocar's Nations Cup

Merc's crazy G63 AMG 6x6 is both exotic and quick

150 Tips from used car expert James Ruppert

THE AUTOCAR NATIONS CUP

Which country produces the best cars? We try to find out in a strictly non-scientific, no-holds-barred knockout contest. **Matt Burt** referees

MATCH 1

FRANCE
Peugeot 205 GTI

MALAYSIA
Proton Satria GTI

MATCH 2

HOLLAND
Spyker C8 Aileron

RUSSIA
Marussia B2

MATCH 3

SWEDEN
Saab 99 Turbo

AUSTRIA
KTM X-Bow

MATCH 4

SLOVENIA
Tushek Renovatio T500

SPAIN
Seat Leon Cupra R

QUARTER-FINAL 1

Winner of match 1

Winner of match 2

QUARTER-FINAL 2

Winner of match 3

Winner of match 4

SEMI-FINAL 1
Winner of q-final 1

Winner of q-final 2

FINAL
Winner of semi-final 1

Welcome to The Autocar Nations Cup, a knockout competition that pitches countries against each other in a bid to determine which one makes the best cars. From the outset, we're more than happy to point out that our competition is a) entirely subjective and b) deeply flawed.

Flawed, because we've chosen just a single representative from each nation and, where possible, we've selected a car that has a deep resonance in automotive history.

So, for example, the Lamborghini Miura appears for Italy because in many ways it set the template for the supercars we know and love today. The E30-specification BMW M3 gets called up to defend Germany's honour in preference to, say, the Volkswagen Golf GTI or Mercedes-Benz C63 AMG because it was a game-changer that's arguably never been surpassed by Munich's 'M' division.

Of course, like any knockout competition, our Nations Cup contains leviathans and minnows, and match-ups that look a little one-sided.

And, naturally, there's a high level of expectation that the cream will rise to the top in the latter stages of the competition. So, without further ado, let battle commence...

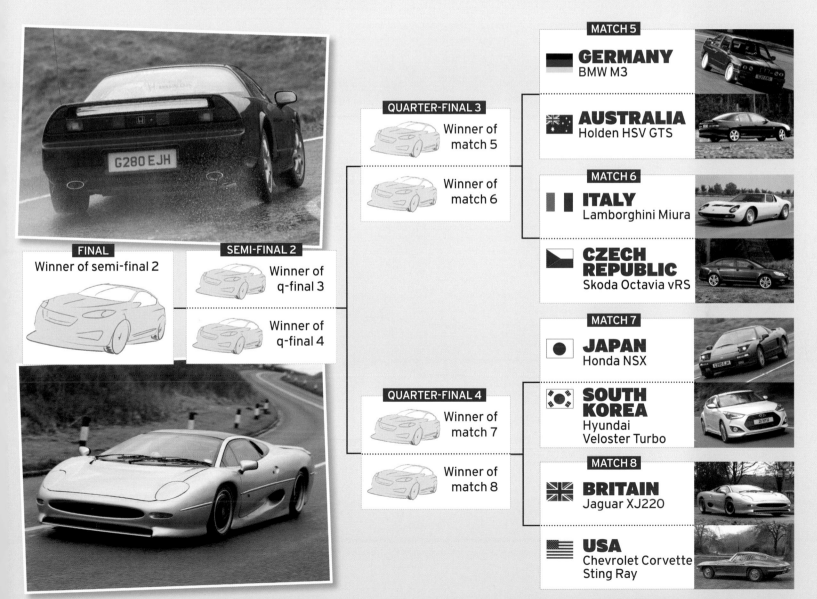

FINAL
Winner of semi-final 2

SEMI-FINAL 2
Winner of q-final 3
Winner of q-final 4

QUARTER-FINAL 3
Winner of match 5
Winner of match 6

QUARTER-FINAL 4
Winner of match 7
Winner of match 8

MATCH 5
GERMANY BMW M3
AUSTRALIA Holden HSV GTS

MATCH 6
ITALY Lamborghini Miura
CZECH REPUBLIC Skoda Octavia vRS

MATCH 7
JAPAN Honda NSX
SOUTH KOREA Hyundai Veloster Turbo

MATCH 8
BRITAIN Jaguar XJ220
USA Chevrolet Corvette Sting Ray

FRANCE
PEUGEOT 205 GTI

IT IS TOO easy to look back on such a car believing its iconic status also made it somehow faultless. This is very far from the case. The very earliest 205 GTI was a rough cut if ever there was one.

Those early cars were merciless. However, so long as you knew it would instantly want to show you where you'd just come from if you lifted off mid-curve, and were as ready with the throttle as the steering to correct it, the car could be made to corner blindingly fast. At the start of its life, this hot hatch was emphatically not for amateurs.

Peugeot soon calmed it down and improved its ride, thus allowing its true talents to shine. Not only was it the best handling hot hatch of its or any other era, but its talent was also complemented by a responsive motor which, once stretched to 1.9 litres, offered ferocious performance too.

It was uncommonly well packaged for its size, had a big and well-shaped boot and was quiet, quite comfortable and notably frugal on long runs.

What you'll believe least is how alive it feels in your hands. Our 1984 test car weighed in at 909kg, an unimaginably low figure for any family hatch today, let alone one with seriously sporting intent. So when you discover it changes direction like a Lotus Elise, remind yourself that it does so because it weighs very little more than an Elise.

PEUGEOT 205 GTI	
Price in 1984	£6520
0-60mph	8.6sec
Top speed	120mph
Economy	29.5mpg
CO$_2$	na
Kerb weight	909kg
Engine layout	4 cyls in line, 1580cc, petrol
Power	105bhp at 6250rpm
Torque	99lb ft at 4000rpm
Gearbox	5-spd manual

PROTON SATRIA GTI	
Price in 2002	£11,995
0-62mph	8.1sec
Top speed	127mph
Economy	32.0mpg
CO2	na
Kerb weight	1065kg
Engine	4 cyls, petrol, 1834cc
Power	138bhp
Torque	119lb ft
Gearbox	5-spd manual

MALAYSIA
PROTON SATRIA GTI

UP AGAINST PEUGEOT'S old-school hot hatch is this more modern attempt from Proton. Malaysia isn't renowned for its performance car heritage, and the fact that the Satria was based around old Mitsubishi underpinnings doesn't bode well.

Some history: after the introduction of the four-door Wira saloon, Proton launched its first-ever three-door hatchback model, the Satria, to the UK in late 1994. Four years later, Proton's collaboration with Lotus gave birth to this Satria GTI. Based on the same three-door body, this 1.8-litre, 138bhp GTI was extensively re-engineered by Lotus and aimed primarily at hardcore car enthusiasts.

The words 'extensively re-engineered' can cover a multitude of sins, but actually the Satra GTI was a major improvement over the uninspiring base model that spawned it.

Mind you, you wouldn't have been convinced simply by looking at the hot Satria. The cheap and cheerful body kit looked like it had come straight from the bargain bin of an aftermarket accessory shop, and the interior was augmented with some faux metal detailing that fooled no-one.

Despite the cosmetic drawbacks, however, the Satria GTI was a moderately involving drive. The hard work carried out by Lotus to tune the

chassis and suspension transformed this mundane hatchback's manners and made it rather good fun on the right road.

And although the engine – a Mitsubishi unit with the turbocharger removed – sounded unpleasantly raucous, it delivered its power from low down in the torque range and provided enough surge to serve up some B-road thrills.

A valiant effort then, and one that retains some cult appeal for knowledgeable hot hatch experts, even if the Proton badge on the front meant it was widely ignored at the time.

THE WINNER IS...

FRANCE
PEUGEOT 205 GTI

A walkover for French flair. The first sporting front-drive hatch did not suffer fools gladly, but was (and still is) massively rewarding if treated with respect.

HOLLAND
SPYKER C8 AILERON

SAY WHAT YOU like about the Dutch, they aren't lacking in flair or commitment. The Spyker C8 Aileron is one of the greatest road car creations to emanate from the fearless men of orange.

Spyker is not, it is fair to surmise, your typical sports car company. To give you an idea what sort of outfit we're talking about, Spyker's motto is 'Nulla tenaci invia est via'. Translated literally this means, 'For the tenacious no road is impassable'. Or, to put it another way, anything in life is possible – so long as you've got the balls.

Yet beneath its strikingly aggressive, aircraft industry influenced styling – complete with jet turbine wheel design and jet engine-inspired air intakes – the C8 is an extremely serious piece of kit. The engine and six-speed semi-auto gearbox are lifted straight out of an Audi S4 and then tuned to suit Spyker's needs, while the mid-engined space frame aluminium chassis were designed and set-up for Spyker by Lotus.

The Aileron is a peculiarly beguiling car, even if it isn't as quick as you'd expect. The good bits include the thunderous noise it makes, the quite extraordinarily exquisite cabin design, the way it steers (which is to say, quite beautifully), and its handling and ride. Oh yes, and its bespoke Louis Vuitton luggage, a 20,000 euro option.

The bad bits are the brakes, which are snatchy but powerful, the slightly unamazing straight line performance and the poor rear visibility.

It's only when you climb in and drive the Aileron that the justification for such pricing becomes apparent, however. Because when you 'get' the Aileron, when you discover how beautifully made it is inside and out, and appreciate just how much craftsmanship has gone into it, the price no longer seems quite so silly.

But only consider buying one if you are very rich and very confident in your own sense of taste – and very happy to be gawped at wherever you go. It would also help if you were as pleasantly unhinged as the good people from Spyker itself seem to be.

SPYKER C8 AILERON	
Price in 2009	£194,000
0-60mph	4.5sec
Top speed	187mph (claimed)
Economy	na
CO$_2$	na
Kerb weight	1560kg
Engine	V8, 4163cc, petrol
Power	395bhp at 7000rpm
Torque	354lb ft at 3500rpm
Gearbox	6-spd semi-auto

MARUSSIA B2	
Price	£88,000 (est)
0-62mph	3.5sec
Top speed	210mph
Economy	na
CO$_2$	na
Kerb weight	1100kg
Engine	V6, 2800cc, turbocharged, petrol
Power	414bhp
Torque	442lb ft at 4000rpm
Gearbox	6-spd automatic

RUSSIA
MARUSSIA B2

PRESUMABLY THE MARUSSIA F1 team, which grew out of Virgin Racing, is designed to draw attention to the Russian company's road car models. That's all fine, apart from the fact that Marussia's two sports car designs to date – firstly the B1 and then a rebodied version called, logically, the B2 – have remained enigmatically low-key.

Indeed, if you're an ardent fan of computer racing games, you might have enjoyed more time behind the wheel of the B2 than most petrolheads, because in 2012 the car had a starring role in a game called 'Need For Speed: World'.

The B1 and B2 are built around an aluminium semi-monocoque structure with front and rear subframes. Cosworth provides a range of engines: depending on your budget and preference, the B2 can be had with a 3.5-litre normally aspirated V6 engine developing 300bhp and 300lb ft of torque,

or a turbocharged 2.8-litre V6 with either 360bhp and 383lb ft or 420bhp and 442lb ft.

While none of those power figures look particularly impressive up against the amount of horses created by established supercar makers, consider that the B2 weighs a scant 1100kg. Power is delivered to the road via a six-speed paddle-shift automatic transmission and the 0-62mph sprint is a claimed (but impressive) 3.5sec.

Inside, the two-seat coupé boasts a high-tech, minimalist cabin in which most of the major controls are operated via large touchscreens.

Marussia Motors is proud of its position as Russia's first sports car manufacturer. The company's founder and president is the colourful Nikolay Fomenko, a man of many skills who has previously been a pilot, racing driver, comic actor and musician.

Apparently a run of 500 Marussia B2s has been constructed by specialist vehicle manufacturer Valmet in Finland and all of them have already been sold to willing customers.

Marussia's next project is rumoured to be an SUV, which could be just the thing to help it break out of obscurity and into the mainstream. Established European and Japanese manufacturers are looking to Russia as a market for huge potential growth over the next decade, but a question mark remains over whether there is room for Russian-derived cars in the global automotive landscape.

THE WINNER IS...

HOLLAND
SPYKER C8 AILERON
The nation that gave us total football wins at total supercar making to knock out the enigmatic Russians. It's true that you might have to be slightly unhinged to buy a Dutch supercar, but you'll be hugely entertained.

SWEDEN
SAAB 99 TURBO

VERY OCCASIONALLY A car comes along which shocks the seen-it-all, driven-them-all Autocar hacks out of their collective complacency. Back in 1978, that's exactly the reaction that the Saab 99 Turbo elicited.

It's not the fastest car that we've ever tested, and it's certainly not one of the best-looking either. But it lived long in the memory because it was such a surprising package, full of interest and excitement.

At the time the 99 Turbo was mechanically unorthodox, but its skilful use of turbocharging to provide lower emissions without compromising power output helped to kick-start a trend among mainstream car makers that's being pursued with an unflinching vigour today.

Even if contemporary rivals could outpace it, the way the Saab delivered its performance is compelling. Like a rollercoaster running downhill, the 99 Turbo just gets faster and faster as the turbocharger boost increases. The turbocharger starts to operate from 1500rpm and comes in with a smooth, insistent build-up of power. There is no throttle lag, and it never gives the impression it is going to run out of power.

There is one caveat: the Turbo is, of course, front-wheel drive and the amount of power and torque transmitted through those wheels makes for some quite twitchy side effects. Under most circumstances, the Saab's front wheels will fight and scrabble as the torque builds, transmitting their disturbance up through the steering wheel. Circumspection is prudent when powering past slower traffic on wet roads...

SAAB 99 TURBO

Price in 1978	£7850
0-62mph	8.9sec
Top speed	122mph
Economy	23.5mpg
CO$_2$	na
Kerb weight	1408kg
Engine	4 cyls turbo, petrol, 1985cc
Power	145bhp at 5000rpm
Torque	174lb ft at 3000rpm
Gearbox	4-spd manual

KTM X-BOW R	
Price in 2011	£64,850
Top speed	144mph
0-62mph	3.9sec
Economy	34.0mpg
CO_2	189g/km
Kerbweight	790kg
Engine	4cyls, 1984cc, turbo petrol
Power	295bhp at 5500rpm
Torque	295lb ft at 3300rpm
Gearbox	6-spd manual

AUSTRIA
KTM X-BOW

THE KTM X-BOW was the product of Austrian motorcycle maker KTM sensing a chill in the air.

Having established itself as a respected maker of off-road and competition motorcycles, KTM dipped its toes more deeply into the road bike market with some predictably hard-edged, high-performance models. However, the slow but relentless decline in the number of motorcycle licences across Europe spurred the firm on to try its engineering hand at building a four-wheeler.

The result is the KTM X-Bow, a roofless, windscreen-less, two seat mid-engined sports car designed for road and track. But it is so outlandish in its design that, even next to the established track-day-inspired oddballs, it looks like it is from another planet.

The X-Bow is powered by a 295bhp 2.0-litre engine from Audi, complete with six-speed gearbox. Structurally, the core of the KTM is an immensely strong carbonfibre tub, much of it exposed, and it's possible to specify ancillary bodywork in matching carbonfibre too.

And of course the KTM X-Bow is predictably fast, not to mention huge fun. Perhaps less predictably is that it is unexpectedly refined, with a supple ride, relatively muted exhausts and a body remarkably free of vibration.

Overall, in standard form at least, the X-Bow feels rapid, grippy, stable and obedient, its chief sensation-generator the denial of a roof and much of a windscreen.

But build speed and confidence and you realise that this is an utterly exhilarating weapon. Turn-in sharpens at speed, spearing the KTM through switchback twists that allow you to feel the car pivoting directly beneath your spine.

It's hard not to fall for the X-Bow's wonderful manners and the flattering way it lets you hone your skills without too many heart-in-mouth moments along the way.

It's no beauty, but it is fascinating to look at and thoroughly well built. This is a terrific track-day machine with remarkably good road manners. But given its price, you've got to love the X-Bow as a piece of engineering and product design as much as you've got to love the driving experience.

THE WINNER IS...

SWEDEN
SAAB 99 TURBO

It shocked Autocar's scribes of the day out of their stupor, and remains a cult classic. The KTM is eye-catching and brave, but didn't revolutionise the car landscape like the Saab.

SLOVENIA
TUSHEK RENOVATIO T500

TUSHEK RENOVATIO T500	
Price in 2012	£241,000
0-62mph	3.7sec
Top speed	193mph
Economy	24.6mpg
CO2	na
Kerb weight	1133kg
Engine	V8, 4163cc, petrol
Power	444bhp at 7900rpm
Torque	316lb ft at 3200rpm
Gearbox	6-spd manual

HERE'S SLOVENIA'S FIRST supercar, the Tushek Renovatio T500. The car is not a totally ground-up design, yet costs more than £240,000. Quite a lot, yes? Yes, but give it a chance.

The Renovatio T500 is the brainchild of company founder and former tin-top racer Aljosa Tušek. It has a tubular spaceframe chassis and power comes from a 4.2-litre Audi RS4 motor that drives the rear wheels via an S5's 6-spd manual gearbox. The body is carbonfibre.

Slovenia doesn't have a rich heritage in supercar manufacture, it's true: but it does have a thriving industry of carbonfibre, composite and titanium specialists that supply certain high-end Italian and German sports car firms.

Tušek works with them all. The Renovatio makes a modest (by supercar standards) 444bhp, but here's the thing: dry, it weighs only 1090kg. Tušek

thinks most supercars aren't particularly suited to track use because they're too heavy. And the Renovatio is pitched at the track-oriented end of the scale, which makes it additionally unusual in supercar circles.

Anything else unusual? Yes. A refreshing lack of over-ambition on the part of the people who build it. They're modest; the claimed top speed starts with a one; the 0-62mph time is a believable (if it gets there in first gear) 3.7sec.

The Renovatio could be one of those cars that's easy to dismiss. Because, well, we've seen this sort of thing before, haven't we? But sometimes there are exceptions, and we're inclined to think and hope that this is one of them.

It's the details, as much as anything. The quality of the body mouldings is excellent. The interior is sweetly finished and the hardware is pretty

straightforward. With fluids this is still only an 1133kg car, so it gets along pretty nicely. Makes a good noise, too, and, because of a lack of sound proofing, a very audible one.

No mistake, there's a thoroughly sorted chassis underneath the T500. That it's relatively light, that its brakes resist fade seemingly interminably, mean that it has a track demeanour more like a GT Porsche or the latest Lotus Exige S than a traditional supercar.

The Renovatio offers something truly unusual in the class: it's a track-biased supercar whose consumables should wear out or overheat less quickly than an alternative that's carrying a few hundred extra kilos.

It's not going get the Italian establishment looking over their shoulders, but it isn't meant to. It's novel and interesting.

SPAIN
SEAT LEON CUPRA R

SEAT LEON CUPRA R	
Price in 2002	£16,995
0-60mph	6.5sec
Top speed	141mph
Economy	23.0mpg
CO₂	211g/km
Kerb weight	1376kg
Engine	4 cyls inline, 1781cc, turbocharged, petrol
Power	210bhp at 5800rpm
Torque	199lb ft at 2100-5000rpm
Gearbox	6-spd manual

BACK IN THE early 2000s, a power struggle was fought out on Britain's roads. The aim of the game was to discover precisely how much grunt you could put through the front wheels of a hot hatch. On the evidence of the Seat Leon Cupra R, the answer would appear to be: quite a lot.

Consider what was on the market at the time that Spain's plucky new entry into the fast hatchback arena arrived. Renault had dropped a 172bhp engine into its tiny Clio, but Honda had trumped that with the UK-built Civic Type-R, which packed 197bhp. The Seat, however, packed 210bhp from a 1.8-litre turbocharged unit, which upped the stakes until the 212bhp Ford Focus RS rocked up a few short months later.

The 'R' suffix means a more focused set-up than the already impressive Leon Cupra. There are stiffer dampers, a lower ride height, a quicker steering rack and uprated brakes. Completing the package are 18in alloys, a front splitter and a subtle rear winglet.

The Leon Cupra R scorches to 60mph in 6.5sec, and possesses the sort of in-gear muscle that helps make it a supreme overtaking tool. The engine itself is not particularly charismatic, though it never becomes harsh, even up to the 6900rpm limiter. Keeping the engine operating in its most effective band between 2500-5500rpm is no great chore, however, because the six-speed gearbox has a slick-enough shift.

Putting more than 200bhp through just the front wheels can so often end in tears, but Seat's engineers did a fine job of ironing out torque steer without resorting to an expensive limited-slip differential as Ford did with the Focus RS. A conventional traction and stability system reins in the power, and brakes individual wheels without imposing on driver enjoyment – just as well considering you can't turn the system off.

Despite an over-firm ride and slightly numb steering, it's hard not to fall for the Cupra R's blend of talents. A valiant effort.

THE WINNER IS...

SPAIN
SEAT LEON CUPRA R

It's fast, good looking and practical as family transport, even if its dynamic talents were ultimately overshadowed by the Ford Focus RS that followed not long afterwards.

BMW M3 (E30)

Price in 1987	£23,128
0-60mph	7.1sec
Top speed	140mph
Test economy	20.3mpg
CO_2	na
Kerb weight	1252kg
Engine	4 cyls inline, 2302cc, petrol
Power	200bhp at 6750rpm
Torque	177lb ft at 4750rpm
Gearbox	5-spd manual

GERMANY
BMW M3

WHY DID ALL the best race tracks evolve from airfields and road networks, and not from modern, computer-aided design?

Simply because some things are better when they're not planned. BMW's motivation for making the M3 was the requirement of Group A touring car rules to build such a car before BMW could race in that category.

If you'd told its engineers that it would go on to spawn many generations and create one of the great automotive icons, they'd probably have suggested you have a little lie down.

As is so often the case with cars conceived purely with driving in mind, it is the M3's authenticity that holds true down the ages. The pedigree of the original E30 M3 is obvious all the way from its race-bred four-cylinder motor and dog-leg five-speed gearbox to those wheel arch blisters, specified not to look good on the King's Road but to accept slick tyres of up to 10in in width.

In many ways it would have been more of a surprise if the M3 had been rubbish to drive. It has a design purity and simplicity of specification that hardly any modern car could match.

The E30 M3 is a wonderfully direct device. That engine, lumpy at idle but sharp and sonorous at the red line, could only be a racing unit, while the gearbox, with its close-stacked ratios and competition pattern, helps fill in the picture.

But it's the way the car handles, combining brilliantly crisp turn-in with unlikely stability and poise, that truly puts you in the seat of a car that, in its short life, won a dozen touring car championships.

Not only does it feel unburstable, but it also inspires great confidence in the driver that the limit is not a danger zone to be avoided or even treated with care or caution; rather it feels like the most natural place in the world for the car.

AUSTRALIA
HOLDEN HSV GTS

HOLDEN HSV GTS	
Price in 1999	£40,590
0-60mph	5.7sec
Top speed	152mph
Test economy	14.3mpg
CO_2	na
Kerb weight	1715kg
Engine	V8, 5700cc, petrol
Power	335bhp at 5600rpm
Torque	349lb ft at 4000rpm
Gearbox	6-spd manual

WHILE EUROPEAN CAR makers were busy trying to transmit drive to the front wheels and fitting transverse four-cylinder engines to their machinery, the Australians were following a surprisingly similar script to the Americans, shoving large displacement V8s into sizeable four-door bodies.

The basic recipe for a fast Aussie saloon just about lives on, and in 1999 the Holden HSV GTS was an effective exponent of the philosophy. Developed from a basic Holden Commodore, itself closely related to the Vauxhall Omega that was more familiar in the UK, the HSV GTS is a legend in its home market, particularly when its creator slotted a mildly detuned version of the Chevrolet Corvette's V8 under the bonnet.

If visual strength was the primary criteria by which hot saloons were judged, the GTS would be the toughest of the lot. Sill extensions and prominent front and rear spoilers give this 4918mm behemoth massive presence on the road.

Mechanically, the Holden is a refreshingly straightforward machine. Up front sits an alloy block, pushrod V8 with a capacity of 5700cc. Maximum power is 335bhp at 5600rpm and torque is 349lb ft at 4000rpm. Front suspension is by conventional struts and coils and the rear end employs trailing arms to harness all that power.

Use no more than 2000rpm off the line and punctuate full throttle with quick gearchanges and the HSV records some deeply impressive times. The magic figure of 100mph comes up in 13.8sec and acceleration remains urgent beyond 120mph. Impressive for a 1715kg saloon.

Curiously the Holden never feels that quick. Perhaps it's the long first gear that runs to 45mph, or just the smooth, linear delivery. No problem with the noise, however. The stirring soundtrack ranges from a moody throb to a NASCAR-style yell.

The gearchange is heavy but rewarding, another enjoyable element of what is a fairly physical driving experience. The ride is crude at times, but

it never feels unruly. Road imperfections filter into the cabin, but excellent front seats do much to isolate occupants from any discomfort.

But the HSV never feels truly wieldy in the way that the BMW M5 does. The driver is always aware of the car's sheer size, so driving quickly on B-roads can be intimidating. It is at its best on smooth, open A-roads where the combination of solid body control and grip makes for real fun.

THE WINNER IS...
GERMANY BMW M3
The big Holden offered startling value for money. However, the E30-spec M3 broke new ground by proving fun is not always about big engines and huge power.

CZECH REPUBLIC
SKODA OCTAVIA VRS

IF YOU'RE LOOKING for a gauge of the car industry's technological progress through the ages, consider that this Skoda Octavia vRS can sprint from a standstill to 62mph in the same 6.7sec as the Lamborghini Miura pictured on the right.

When it came to market in the spring of 2006, this second-generation spicy Skoda was bigger, faster and better to drive than its game-changing predecessor. It borrows its styling cues from the previous model, but under the skin it uses the acclaimed VW Golf Mk5 platform, complete with multi-link rear suspension.

There are changes under the bonnet too. Gone is the old 1.8-litre turbo unit, replaced by the Golf GTI's 1984cc direct injection turbocharged four-cylinder engine.

On the road the new engine's blend of lag-free power at low revs and top-end zeal is a world away from the flat power delivery of old. Whereas the old car needed 9.1sec to travel from 50-70mph in fifth, the new model takes just 6.1sec. At the time, it was sufficient to keep it near the front of the hot-hatch crowd; in a straight-line race only the snarling Vauxhall Astra VXR was quicker.

Over B-roads the benefit of the Octavia's multi-link suspension is immediately evident. In cold, wet and greasy conditions, a well-driven vRS covers ground impressively quickly. The talents of the chassis are similar to the GTI's – accurate steering, mid-corner adjustability and confidence-inspiring grip. Of the two, the Octavia provides a more compliant ride, but its steering is less weighty, the turn-in less sharp and the cornering less incisive.

The second iteration of the Octavia vRS was still the cheapest and most versatile hot hatch when it went on sale, and it remains an excellent used buy today. The margin of advantage over its rivals was not as great as when the first-generation car appeared and sprinkled some star dust on Skoda's reputation. In estate form a used Octavia vRS makes great sense; for the money, nothing can match its combination of space and pace.

SKODA OCTAVIA VRS	
Price in 2006	£17,500
0-62mph	6.7sec
Top speed	143mph
Test economy	23.8mpg
CO_2	207g/km
Kerb weight	1430kg
Engine	4 cyls inline, 1984cc, petrol
Power	197bhp at 5100rpm
Torque	206lb ft at 1800-5000rpm
Gearbox	6-spd manual

LAMBORGHINI MIURA	
Price in 1970	£10,860
0-62mph	6.7sec
Top speed	173mph
Test economy	13.4mpg
CO_2	na
Kerb weight	1300kg
Engine	V12, 3929cc, petrol
Power	370bhp at 7700rpm
Torque	286lb ft at 4750rpm
Gearbox	5-spd manual

ITALY
LAMBORGHINI MIURA

REPRESENTING ITALY IS the car that was, arguably, the world's first supercar, although some might blanch at that suggestion. Certainly, when the Lamborghini Miura was unveiled at the Geneva motor show in 1966, the world swooned in much the same way as it had five years earlier when Jaguar had used the same event to launch the E-type.

The Miura was nothing short of a revolution, with a V12 mounted not only behind the driver but transversely to boot. As for looks, the fact that Nuccio Bertone, Marcello Gandini and Giorgetto Giugiaro all claimed to have had a hand in it probably tells you all you need to know.

But the Miura was deeply flawed. The cabin was an ergonomic disaster, with a driving position best suited to residents of Planet of the Apes. Over-the-shoulder visbility was negligible, the clutch was merciless on your left thigh, you needed both hands to engage reverse (really) and God help anyone

who parked their Miura on even a slight incline, expecting the handbrake to keep it there.

Even once you were under way on clear, dry roads, the Miura remained an acquired taste. Despite heavy steering and a poor lock, it was a reasonable drive unless you started exploring the limit of its tall 205/70 VR15 Pirelli tyres. Then you would discover the hard way that the science of engineering mid-engined road cars was in its infancy. It was only when the final SV version was launched in 1971 that Lamborghini really got on top of the handling issues.

But the Miura was a car you couldn't stay mad at for long, even with its cramped cabin, dodgy build quality, hideous running costs and questionable handling. If the looks didn't make you fall in love with it, the engine would.

Back in 1970 there were no catalytic converters and, in Italy at least, no silencing requirement

either. Fed by four triple-choke Weber carburetors, the 3.9-litre V12's call provided the best way ever to go deaf. And if the performance figures seem rather lame by modern standards, remember this was a car with little torque, probably less power than claimed and a very slow gearshift.

THE WINNER IS...

ITALY
LAMBORGHINI MIURA

The Octavia vRS makes a compelling case for itself, but the Miura is a work of art and, in its day, was technically ground-breaking. It's not the greatest supercar, but it's difficult to think of a more influential one.

JAPAN
HONDA NSX

TO UNDERSTAND JUST how frightened of the Honda NSX the European supercar manufacturers were prior to its arrival, you need first to appreciate its context. It came at a time when Japanese car makers were redefining luxury cars (Lexus), small cars (Nissan Micra) and sports cars (Mazda MX-5). The real fear was that the Japanese now possessed the ability to entirely eclipse anything that was coming out of Europe.

So imagine just how jittery things must have been at Porsche, Ferrari and others when details of the NSX started leaking out.

Crafted from aluminium, with forged wishbones, an engine with variable valve and intake control, built in a bespoke factory and developed by Ayrton Senna… the writing appeared to be on the wall and it was in Japanese.

And the Honda NSX was not a disappointment.

On the contrary, the way it blended searing performance and pussycat handling into a package as easy to drive as a Civic was genuinely shocking.

We didn't know then that, in sales terms, the NSX would prove a failure. The badge lay at the heart of that: it was a Honda, a concept that prospects with Ferrari-driving chums proved unable to accept in sufficient quantities. Only now, two decades since its launch, is Honda creating a successor.

HONDA NSX	
Price in 1990	£52,000
0-60mph	5.8sec
Top speed	162mph
Economy	19.6mpg
CO_2	na
Kerb weight	1567kg
Engine	V6, 2977cc, petrol
Power	270bhp at 7100rpm
Torque	210lb ft at 5300rpm
Gearbox	5-spd manual

HYUNDAI VELOSTER TURBO SE	
Price	£21,995
0-62mph	8.4secs
Top speed	133mph
Economy	40.9mpg
CO_2	157g/km
Kerb weight	1313kg
Engine	4 cyls turbo, petrol, 1591cc
Power	184bhp at 5500rpm
Torque	195lb ft at 1500-4500rpm
Gearbox	6-spd manual

SOUTH KOREA
HYUNDAI VELOSTER TURBO

HYUNDAI HAS MADE huge strides in the car market over the last few years, performing a metamorphosis from a manufacturer of cheap and cheerful cars to a thoroughly credible automotive heavyweight. So it was only a matter of time before the South Koreans decided to sprinkle a little stardust on their model line-up by producing some performance variants.

Compared to the standard Veloster, this Turbo version features chassis modifications alongside the first application of the firm's new 1.6-litre T-GDI engine. It has a twin-scroll turbocharger and represents a 33 per cent increase in power and 59 per cent increase in torque over the naturally aspirated engine.

The Veloster Turbo retains the standard car's MacPherson strut front and coupled torsion beam rear suspension set-up, but the damping rates have been increased. The much-maligned power steering system has been modified, too.

If the standard Veloster lacked the performance expected from the small coupé, the Turbo goes a long way to address that. Keep the engine in the peak torque zone and the engine is smooth, if lacking the rorty engine note promised by the large twin tailpipes. Beyond peak torque the engine becomes coarse, so it is more satisfying to short-shift than hold on to a gear. The claimed 8.4sec 0-62mph time isn't exceptional, but it allows rapid progress to be made.

Tweaks to the steering mean it's free from the inconsistencies the standard car was berated for, although there's a vagueness and lightness around the dead-ahead. When pushing on, it lacks the delicacy of the best, but it's still the sharpest Hyundai by some stretch.

The biggest praise is reserved for the retuned suspension setup. Front and rear damping rates have been increased to deliver a planted feel and a well-judged ride.

Although a similarly priced Vauxhall Astra GTC or Volkswagen Scirocco offers a greater depth of dynamic ability, this Hyundai is a solid statement of intent from the South Korean manufacturer. Despite the significant progress it has already made in terms of its products and reputation, don't expect it to let up for a second.

THE WINNER IS...

JAPAN
HONDA NSX

South Korea is consistently producing the goods these days, but Japan triumphs in this contest. Overall the NSX is remembered not simply as one of the best supercars, but as one of the most important too.

USA
CHEVROLET CORVETTE STING RAY

IF EVER THERE was a sports car designed for America, where the roads are long and straight and corners an occasional curiosity, the Corvette Sting Ray is it. With its transverse leaf spring suspension, drum brakes and 360bhp, the car was hardly a menace, on paper at least.

Yet our 1963 road test of the car is littered with warnings of it swapping ends at 80mph in the wet in a straight line, being deflected off course by rubbishy tyres at 140mph and of the steering

becoming 'of little assistance' during cornering, such was the car's throttle sensitivity.

At the time, we said the Sting Ray was 'a curious mixture of concepts of what a genuine Gran Turismo car should be'. Despite a body shape that looks efficient, our 1964 test car topped out at 146.5mph, compared with 152.3mph for the Aston Martin DB4 GT Zagato and 152.7mph for the Jaguar E-type coupé, each of which was armed with a less-powerful engine.

For all its outlandish looks and sledgehammer performance, the Corvette was, is and always will be the supercar of the people, even if in the main those people live on the other side of the Atlantic.

Running parallel to, and inseparable from, the story of the Corvette is the story of its most popular engine, the small-block V8. It has provided an evocative soundtrack for generations of American sports car enthusiasts, and its influence on car culture on that side of the Atlantic is indelible.

CHEVROLET CORVETTE STING RAY

Price in 1963	£3432
0-60mpg	6.5sec
Top speed	147mph
Economy	20.5mpg
CO_2	na
Kerb weight	1473kg
Engine	V8, 5363cc, petrol
Power	360bhp at 6000rpm
Torque	352lb ft at 4000rpm
Gearbox	4-spd manual

JAGUAR XJ220	
Price in 1993	£403,000
0-60mph	3.6sec
Top speed	213mph (claimed)
Economy	13.8mpg
CO$_2$	na
Kerb weight	1456kg
Engine	V6, 3500cc, turbocharged, petrol
Power	542bhp at 7200rpm
Torque	475lb ft at 4500rpm
Gearbox	5-spd manual

BRITAIN
JAGUAR XJ220

THE XJ220 HAS to be the unluckiest supercar ever created. Jaguar got into the supercar business just as grim global economic conditions ensured that everyone else was getting out. At £403,000, the XJ220 was ferociously expensive but it was also, for a short time, the ultimate supercar.

Yet, even as we were driving this British supercar we had one eye on the next, because we knew that whatever the XJ220 did, the McLaren F1 was going to do it a whole lot faster even than that.

And so it did. We were stunned by the XJ220's 0-100mph time of 7.9sec, but only until the McLaren did it in 6.3sec less than a year later.

And while we were able to record acceleration times up to 170mph, the F1 blew straight past 200mph. It was in a different league, and the XJ220 was duly humbled.

But remove the context of time and timing and what remains of the XJ220? Well, you couldn't see out of it, the engine sounded like gravel being poured into a blender and it needed careful management in the wet, but despite all that we still remember it with an unalloyed fondness.

On the right road, the Jaguar XJ220 would take you to places no other road car had hitherto visited. And as for road presence, we don't think you'd move over any quicker if a Bugatti Veyron appeared in your mirrors. Every one of Autocar's testers who travelled in the Jaguar at the time emerged with a completely revised concept of the outer limits of road car capability. The fact that it gave us a standard by which all other fast cars could be compared should be justification enough. It is British too, and we should be proud of that.

THE WINNER IS...

BRITAIN
JAGUAR XJ220

In the US, the Corvette is the closest thing to a national monument that a car can be, but the Jag wins a close contest. For a short while at least it could say it was the fastest production car on Earth.

QUARTER-FINALS

QUARTER-FINAL 1

HOLLAND
SPYKER C8 AILERON
VS
FRANCE
PEUGEOT 205 GTI

ON PAPER, YOU'D fancy an expensive, exclusive supercar to prevail over a basic-but-fast go-kart on wheels, but you'd be reckoning without the captivating allure of the best French hot hatch of all time.

By the time the 1.9-litre, 130bhp version arrived in 1987, Peugeot had optimised the development and design to a point that, some say, has never been beaten. Today, the 205 GTI remains as involving to drive as it did when Thatcher was in power, and that makes it a runaway winner of this round.

QUARTER-FINAL 2

SPAIN
SEAT LEON CUPRA R
VS
SWEDEN
SAAB 99 TURBO

THE SPANISH CAR ruffled a few feathers among its contemporaries, even giving its stable-mate the Volkswagen Golf GTI a few sleepless nights. Its combination of good value and raw pace means that even now, more than a decade on, it holds plenty of appeal among hot hatch aficionados.

Whereas the Leon Cupra R is a very good performance hatch, however, the original Saab 99 Turbo was a groundbreaking one, and the technology under the bonnet was a portent of what was to come for the automotive world.

WINNER FRANCE PEUGEOT 205 GTI

WINNER SWEDEN SAAB 99 TURBO

QUARTER-FINAL 3
ITALY
LAMBORGHINI MIURA
VS
GERMANY
BMW M3

WHILE THE LAMBORGHINI can lay claim to being the first authentic supercar, the E30 M3 set a new standard when it appeared in the late 1980s.

Although the Miura possesses some of the most captivating curves ever committed to paper by Italian designers, as well as a spine-tingling engine note, it loses out to Munich's machine when it comes to pure driver involvement. Few cars of any shape or size can match its design purity or single-minded sense of purpose.

QUARTER-FINAL 4
BRITAIN
JAGUAR XJ220
VS
JAPAN
HONDA NSX

AT THE TIME of its launch, Autocar rated the XJ220 as 'the finest-handling supercar we have ever driven'. Others have reset the benchmarks, but in 1993 the XJ220 made all the usual measures of performance look faintly ridiculous.

However, this contest falls to Honda. Whereas the Big Cat's star has faded slightly, that of its Japanese rival still glows as brightly now as it did in 1990. As well built and usable as a Porsche 911 and as adroit as a Lotus, the NSX is a breathtaking engineering feat and deliciously driveable to boot.

WINNER GERMANY BMW M3

WINNER JAPAN HONDA NSX

SEMI-FINALS

JAPAN
HONDA NSX
VS
GERMANY
BMW M3

TWO CARS RENOWNED for their spectacular engineering meet in the first semi-final. When we road tested the M3 back in 1987, we said: "With 200bhp to play with in a car weighing 1252kg, performance is naturally one of the M3's strong suits, but while 200bhp from a 2.3-litre engine might seem like the recipe for a very peaky power delivery, this proves far from the case".

Of the NSX we raved: "It is impossible to doubt this car's credentials. From the forged aluminium double wishbones to the quad-cam, 24-valve, 3.0-litre V6, this is a tour de force worthy of the greatest names in motoring".

It's difficult to remember now but when the NSX was unveiled at the 1989 Chicago motor show, it was almost expected that supercars would be difficult and cumbersome devices to drive, with patchy reliability and no day-to-day usability. Honda's entry into the supercar market changed all that, with light controls, good visibility, and bulletproof mechanicals. It wasn't long before other manufacturers followed suit.

Despite that, it's the M3 that slips through to the final by the narrowest of margins. The car's race-bred DNA was perfectly distilled into one of the greatest road cars ever built, and one stint behind the wheel is enough to deduce that the cult following it engenders is thoroughly justified.

WINNER
GERMANY BMW M3

SWEDEN
SAAB 99 TURBO
VS
FRANCE
PEUGEOT 205 GTI

THE SAD DEMISE of Saab hasn't clouded Trollhättan's reputation as the creator of some of the most satisfying and technologically ingenious vehicles in automotive history.

Despite a fairly high price tag for its day (it was on a par with the Porsche 924 and BMW 528i) the 99 Turbo offered a great deal for the outlay. Its Scandinavian heritage meant it was engineered very well and offered a roomy hatchback bodyshape and thrilling performance, which was still a rare combination back in the late 1970s.

The 99 Turbo wasn't left wanting for pace, although its achievements were put into sharp focus by the 205 GTI and other performance hatches that followed.

The hot hatch genre has been around for more than three decades now, but never has it created an act more difficult to follow than the 205 GTI. It was the fact that such a great driving experience came wrapped up in a brilliantly practical and great-looking package that proved so utterly unanswerable.

Fun on the right roads, quiet and comfortable on the wrong ones, Peugeot's pocket rocket hit the sweet spot right in the bullseye. It's combination of light weight, strong performance and barely believable handling swept all rivals aside, just as it leaves the turbocharged Saab trailing in its wake in this competition.

WINNER
FRANCE PEUGEOT 205 GTI

FINAL

GERMANY BMW M3 VS

THE AUTOMOTIVE WORLD has moved on a great deal from the 1980s, when our two finalists were in their pomp. Nevertheless, there is plenty that today's car designers could learn from the purity of purpose that BMW and Peugeot instilled in two of their greatest-ever creations.

The M3 possesses almost double the power of the 205 GTI, and can sprint from a standstill to 60mph 1.5sec quicker, but in many ways the two machines are cut from similar cloth. Despite being old, noisy and not very fast by modern standards, they still feel immediate, alive and relevant, and are still exciting and edgy to drive.

Neither car was engineered for the faint-hearted; less-sorted early examples of the 205 GTI are notorious for their willingness to oversteer dramatically should the driver decide to lift off the throttle in the middle of a corner.

The M3's driving experience is surprisingly benign for a car that was born on the race circuit, but it is also scarily rapid by the standards of the day. Offsetting that is a quite delicious amount of feel from the steering, and from the rear axle when the car is loaded in a corner.

So why does the Peugeot win this contest by the most slender of margins? Because we know now what we could not possibly have known when the 205 GTI first appeared: pound for pound, it is challenged only by the Golf GTI for the title of the best hot hatch the world has known.

FRANCE
PEUGEOT 205 GTI

WINNER
FRANCE PEUGEOT 205 GTI

McLaren will keep the new P1 exclusive by building 375 examples

SUPERCAR TITANS GO HEAD-TO-HEAD

This year the F1 rivalry between McLaren and Ferrari spilled over into the road car arena. **Mark Tisshaw** describes the big fight

Maranello says all 499 LaFerraris have already been sold

The drivers may change in Formula 1, the road cars may come and go, but the rivalry between Ferrari and McLaren never changes. As with all great rivalries – think India-Pakistan in cricket, Rangers-Celtic in football, or Senna-Prost in motor sport – it can flare up and come under the most public of scrutiny.

And in 2013, the rivalry between Ferrari and McLaren did just that

after the pair revealed the two most technically advanced road cars in history within an hour of each other at the Geneva motor show.

In the red corner is LaFerrari and in the orange it's the McLaren P1. On paper the pair are incredibly closely matched; both are close to £1million in price, both are being built in strictly limited numbers (375 P1s, 499 LaFerraris) and feature technology derived from the manufacturers'

respective F1 cars for very similar performance figures.

Both machines have similar mission statements: to be the best driver's car in the world, rather than necessarily the fastest. But how they go about reaching that goal is where the key differences start to emerge.

Let's start with LaFerrari. The name itself is quite a statement. Forget any other road car that's been produced by Maranello over the past

six or so decades, this new car's name claims it is 'the Ferrari', full stop.

To make the Ferrari, the Prancing Horse has built its remarkable new machine from scratch. At its heart is a mid-mounted 6.3-litre V12 engine, which produces a colossal 790bhp. But the performance potential does not end there, because the engine is mated to an F1-derived electric boost system that pushes LaFerrari's power output to a prodigious 950bhp. →

McLaren has equipped its new machine with adjustable suspension

McLaren has packed its hypercar with F1-inspired tech

The P1 has a rear wing that works like a drag reduction system

The headline power figure is one the McLaren P1 cannot live with. It combines a twin-turbocharged 3.8-litre V8 engine (derived from its smaller MP4-12C supercar) with 727bhp to a kinetic energy recovery system (KERS) that endows the P1 with a total 903bhp. As mightily impressive as this sounds, in this high-stakes game of automotive Top Trumps, it is one-nil to Ferrari.

Both hypercars are built around carbonfibre tubs. The Ferrari's is all-new and the McLaren's is a development of that seen in the MP4-12C, as with the engine.

The 'borrowing and improving' approach of McLaren's is one that clearly grates with Ferrari boss Luca di Montezemolo, who told *Autocar*: "The McLaren is not a 100 per cent new car. I wanted a design [for LaFerrari] that has nothing to do with any of our cars, past or present."

Don't get fooled by the Ferrari chief's comments that the P1 is just an MP4-12C in drag. It has at least as much in common with McLaren's F1 car as it does with the 12C, such is the amount of motor sport-derived active aerodynamics on the car. Indeed, McLaren concedes that the P1 is a car designed as much by the air as by a designer's sketch book. It is penned in the same way as an F1 car.

The active aero technology includes a movable rear wing that pops out of the rear section of the car. Air is channelled from the front of the car, underneath it and onto the wing to increase downforce in a setup that is similar to F1's drag reduction system (DRS). A double rear diffuser further increases downforce.

Another weapon in the McLaren's armoury, one which LaFerrari cannot match, is adjustable suspension. In Track mode the P1 sits almost as low

F1 legend Fernando Alonso helped to develop LaFerrari

Driving position will be tailored around each customer

LaFerrari weighs 1255kg before fluids are added

as a F1 car, just millimetres from the ground, so if you want to negotiate a speed bump you have to raise the car by deploying 'lift' mode.

All this adjustability and advanced aerodynamics points to a car that becomes more rewarding and offers more grip and performance the harder you drive it, much like an F1 car. Put simply, F1 cars just don't work at slow speeds. How McLaren makes sure the P1 can be driven

by mere mortals who aren't Jenson Button is one the greatest challenges.

What the Ferrari does have in addition to vast amounts of power is a great deal of pedigree from decades of making some of the finest supercars the world has ever seen. And that pedigree is oozing from LaFerrari. It weighs less than the P1, although the official given figure of 1255kg doesn't include fluids, whereas McLaren's claim of 1400kg

for the P1 is a kerb weight. LaFerrari also features a host of F1-derived active aerodynamic technology of its own, a bespoke driving position that will be moulded around the owner akin to a single-seater racer, and a development team that included Fernando Alonso on its staff. And it just looks stunning in red, right?

Perhaps this a rivalry where both end up winners: everyone needs a rival to keep them on their toes,

and you can be sure LaFerrari and P1 have had an extra 10 per cent squeezed out of their potential because the boys from Maranello and Woking knew all along that there is a formidable opponent to conquer.

There is another winner we already know: the customer. If you're wealthy enough to buy one of these million-pound machines, chances are you can afford to buy them both. You lucky so and so. ◙

LaFerrari vs McLaren P1

£1,040,000 £866,000

ENGINE LAYOUT
V12, 6262cc, petrol
V8, 3799cc, twin-turbo, petrol

GEARBOX
7-spd dual-clutch auto
7-spd dual-clutch auto

POWER (BHP)
950
903

TORQUE (lb ft)
715
664

HOW MANY WILL BE MADE?
499
375

DRY WEIGHT
1255kg

HEIGHT 1116MM

WHEELBASE 2650MM

LENGTH 4702MM

WIDTH 1992MM

KERB WEIGHT
1400KG

WHEELBASE 2670MM

HEIGHT 1170MM

WIDTH 1946MM

LENGTH 4590MM

TOP SPEED
- NOT QUOTED
- 218MPH (LIMITED)

POWER PER TONNE (EST)
- 756BHP
- 647BHP

TORQUE PER TONNE
- 569LB FT
- 475LB FT

0-62MPH
- UNDER 3.0SEC
- UNDER 3.0SEC

0-124MPH
- UNDER 7.0SEC
- UNDER 7.0SEC

0-186MPH
- 15.5SEC
- UNDER 17.0SEC

THE MOST FRUGAL PRODUCTION CAR EVER

The cutting-edge hybrid VW XL1 has been a long time in development, but its promise of 313mpg is now reality

The XL1 is a hyper-economical, carbonfibre, gullwing-doored two-seater that is the culmination of more than a decade of engineering effort at Volkswagen. This started with the turn-of-the-century vision of Ferdinand Piech (now chairman of the VW supervisory board) to build a production car capable of covering 100km on a litre of fuel, or 282mpg.

The first concept was the 2002 L1, which featured a carbonfibre body, tandem seating, a side-hinged canopy and a single-cylinder 8bhp engine.

The car weighed just 290kg and the company claimed fuel economy of 0.99 litres per 100km, or 285mpg. The second-generation L1 was shown in autumn 2009. This had a hybrid transmission that combined a two-cylinder diesel engine with an electric motor.

However, the problem with making the L1 production-ready was not just the uncivilised tandem seating and the aircraft-style side-hinged roof canopy but also the issue of test requirements.

Less than two years after the second-generation L1, VW showed the

XL1 in the form of a series of driveable prototypes at the Qatar motor show. VW had taken a huge leap with the concept by retaining the two-cylinder hybrid drivetrain but completely rethinking the body design.

The final design is based around a supercar-style carbonfibre-reinforced plastic (CFRP) monocoque passenger cell, with the passenger's seat staggered behind the driver's seat. This clever arrangement reduces the amount of shoulder room needed, allowing the body to be as narrow as possible for aerodynamic reasons.

Crash protection front and rear is provided by large extruded aluminium crash boxes and the mid-mounted powertrain is hung off the rear aluminium subframe. The whole assembly weighs just 230kg. To make for easier access across the wide sills, the XL1 has large gullwing doors that cut right into the roof. If you end up upside down in the XL1, explosive bolts release the doors.

The XL1 is 3.88m long, just 1.65m wide and 1.15m tall – which makes it nearly 100mm shorter than a Polo, around 20mm narrower and close to

300mm lower. These dimensions are, of course, at the maximum points. In reality, the XL1 looks tiny, not just because it is so low but also because the body tapers away to the classic teardrop shape, with the rear wheels enclosed by the bodywork. It has a drag coefficient of just 0.189, surely a world record for a production car.

The front suspension is made up of double wishbones, the rear a semi-trailing link system. The brake discs are made of lightweight ceramic and the wheels are magnesium. The front wheels are almost motorcycle slim.

Behind the passenger cell is the two-cylinder hybrid drivetrain. In effect half of an existing 1.6-litre turbodiesel, tweaked and fitted with a balancer shaft, it develops 50bhp and the electric motor gives 27bhp. Both drive through a seven-speed DSG gearbox. The 5.5kWh lithium-ion battery pack is mounted in the front of the car, ahead of the passenger's feet.

The XL1 can run on diesel only, electric only or, in boost mode, a combination of the two. During boost mode, the two motors generate a maximum of 68bhp and 103lb ft of torque. The XL1's top speed is governed to 99mph and it can hit 62mph from rest in a claimed 12.7sec.

It takes a bit of effort to get into the XL1. The sills are very wide and the seats very low, but once you're inside it is very comfortable indeed. The view ahead is panoramic, while the view directly behind is non-existent because there's no rear window. The rear-view mirrors have been replaced by what looks like a pair of iPhone →

At a steady 62mph, the XL1 requires just 8bhp to make progress. It also feels entirely happy at 75mph

There's no back window; cameras show rear view

←screens mounted in the door trims; the XL1 is the first production car in the world to have rear-view cameras in place of conventional mirrors.

The driving environment is superb. The thin seats are very comfortable – the backs are fixed, but the whole seat can be re-angled – and the driving position is naturally long-legged. The dashboard, which is made from a wood-based fibre and is just 1.4mm thick, is a model of clarity and tasteful execution.

Rather than take the obvious route of designing a suitably sci-fi cockpit, VW has stayed with conventional dials and switchgear. There's an effortlessly classy feel to this all-black finish highlighted by thin chrome bezels. The steering wheel is lovely, too. There's decent practicality to the XL1 thanks to the deep boot space – good for a pair of sizeable weekend bags – positioned in the tail end.

Twist the key, put the shift lever into 'D' and the car hums away on battery power. Straight away you are aware of the different sensations that come from a car built around a carbonfibre monocoque. There's a slight hollowness and resonance to the sounds transmitted into the cabin. The still-cold diesel engine

fires up as I accelerate, and the noise is alarming. A kind of empty, reverberating metallic thrum fills the cabin, something that would have sounded like the death rattle in a conventional four-pot engine.

Perhaps the best way of summarising the XL1 is that it is exceptional on the motorway, highly competent on good A-roads and agreeably flawed in town. On a straight road, the XL1 is very stable and straight-running, with easily enough power to keep up with traffic flow. It is surprisingly comfortable and quiet on decent roads. The steering is accurate and the swiftness and seamlessness of the engine cutting in and out is very impressive – even if it is relatively vocal, especially when completely cold. Even the smallest incline can be quickly detected by the XL1 and the engine is almost instantly spun up to assist the electric motor and battery pack.

In town, the story is slightly less happy. The ride can be a little brittle and the unassisted steering takes some getting used to. It's quite hard, say, to whip around a mini-roundabout because the steering weights up considerably mid-turn. The brakes feel a little dead and are also quite

noisy, but that's a consequence of the lightweight ceramic brake discs. And you have to move around in the seat to try to see properly at junctions. Leaning forward to look around the A-pillars can cause you to bang your head on the low windscreen surround. Yes, it takes a little thought to drive around on narrow streets, but the learning curve is likely to be short.

On the motorway, though, the XL1 is supreme. Despite its tiny footprint and in heavy rain, the XL1 is rock-steady on the motorway and completely unruffled by passing lorries. It runs

very straight and true, requiring virtually no steering corrections. At a steady 62mph, the XL1 requires just 8bhp to make progress – an indication of the car's remarkably low rolling and air resistance. It also feels entirely happy at 75mph and above and during brisk overtaking manoeuvres.

On a longer test drive, which included crossing a mountain range, the most economical drivers achieved a real 188mpg. On a long motorway run, there's surely potential for 200mpg. Overall, the XL1 is quite an unusual experience, but a very

XL1's cabin retains a conventional layout for its controls and instruments

The XL has a super-slippery Cd of 0.189

The XL1 is a true landmark machine that points the way to the future

satisfying one for any driver who appreciates the brilliant engineering behind the car.

Whatever VW charges for the the 250 production examples of the XL1 that are to be hand-made at the Karmann factory in Osnabruck, there's no doubt that it will make a huge loss on the project, but that is hardly the point. It is a technological marvel.

The XL1 is a true landmark machine that points the way to the future. Its engine will help to create a new powertrain for plug-in hybrid cars based on VW's MQB architecture.

The design and layout of the XL1's powertrain will be scaled up with a four-cylinder engine and a more robust six-speed dual-clutch automatic transmission to cope with up to 300lb ft, and a 9kWh battery.

The first car to get the powertrain will be the A3 hybrid. It should have a range of 30 miles on electric power alone and, according to VW's research and development chief Ulrich Hackenberg, be capable of returning between 177mpg and 188mpg.

Those super-early adopters who can't wait will adore the XL1 – and the chance to hone their driving skills enough to achieve more than 200mpg.
HILTON HOLLOWAY

LET THERE BE LIGHTNESS

The XL1 weighs 795kg. Of this, the entire drive unit, including the battery, weighs 227kg, the running gear 153kg, the electrical system 105kg and other 'equipment' 80kg. The body – mostly carbonfibre-reinforced plastic – weighs 230kg, including the doors and 3.2mm-thick front windscreen. Precisely 21.3 per cent of the XL1, or 169kg, consists of CFRP. VW says only 23.2 per cent (184kg) of the XL1 is constructed from steel and iron. The rest of its weight is distributed among various other polymers (for example, polycarbonate side windows), metals, natural fibres, process materials and electronics.

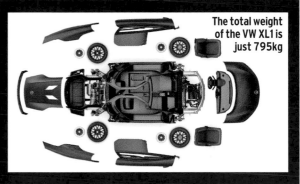

The total weight of the VW XL1 is just 795kg

The gullwing doors swing out of the way to ease the awkward access over the wide sills

VOLKSWAGEN XL1

Price	na
0-62mph	12.7sec
Top speed	99mph (governed)
Economy	313mpg (NEDC)
CO$_2$	21g/km
Kerb weight	795kg
Engine	2 cyls in line, 800cc, turbodiesel; electric motor
Installation	Mid, transverse, RWD
Power	68bhp
Torque	103lb ft
Gearbox	7-spd dual-clutch auto
Fuel tank	10 litres
Wheels	15in (f), 16in (r)
Tyres	115/80 R15 (f), 145/55 R16 (r)

MANUFACTURER'S CLAIMED FIGURES

1964

LESS THAN 20 years after the end of WW2, private car ownership has started to explode across the country. Motorway construction has been underway for five years and the ancient steam-powered rail network has been culled to reduce huge losses.

There's a sense of modernity in the air: the pop music revolution is well underway and the space race has begun, with the US aiming to land men on the Moon by the end of the decade.

Modernity also hits politics. The Conservatives have been in office for 13 years but the tweed-clad ruling party gives way to the self-consciously modern Labour leader Harold Wilson and his promise of an economy forged in the 'White Heat of Technology.' Britain, while becoming less poor, is also still racked by strikes that make a major contribution to the stop-start progress of the UK-based car industry.

■ Experimental 'yellow box' road markings are introduced to London.

■ 6933 people were killed on UK roads in 1963, the government reveals.

■ The first-generation Ford Mustang (right) is unveiled.

■ The Lord Mayor of London demands a Monday-Friday 7am-7pm ban on lorries from the City of London. The same argument over lorries will still be raging 50 years later.

■ The UK motorway network has reached 290 miles in length, up from 81 miles in 1960.

■ A general 50mph Summer speed limit, intended to reduce accidents on motorways, is dropped.

JANUARY | FEBRUARY | MARCH | APRIL | MAY | JUNE

■ Paddy Hopkirk and co-driver Henry Liddon win the 1964 Monte Carlo rally in a Mini Cooper S (below right), cementing the tiny car's growing reputation.

■ Commercial vehicle maker Leyland causes a fuss when it decides to sell buses to Cuba, breaking the US trade embargo on the communist nation.

■ The Mini becomes the UK's best-selling car after four years on sale.

■ The somewhat old-school Austin-Healey 3000 is launched.

■ The Beatles appear on American TV for the first time in front of 73 million viewers.

■ BMC announces that it built 43,661 sports cars in 1963. Of those, 36,846 were exported.

■ As car use rises, the first calls for 'road pricing' are reported in Autocar. The British Road Federation calls for motorway building to be extended.

■ The Ministry of Transport orders an inquiry when an AC Cobra hits 183mph on the M1, as part of a test ahead of the Le Mans 24 Hours (below). AC's Charles Hurlock admits discomfort at the incident but says no UK track can accommodate such tests.

MOTORING

Ever wondered what the world of motoring was like in previous generations? **Hilton Holloway** is your guide on a whistle-stop tour through 50 years of British cars

- It's announced that a completely new system of road signage will be rolled out across the UK from 1965. It's based on the modern and ultra-clear motorway designs developed by Kinneir and Calvert for the roads.
- The new Forth Road Bridge opens in Scotland.

- The Austin 1800 is voted European Car of The Year.
- The Labour government starts a campaign against 'Drink Driving' and the first calls for seat belts (left) to become a legal requirement are reported by Autocar.

- First flight of the space-skipping SR71 spy plane (right).
- The Labour government introduces tolls on the Severn Bridge.

JULY AUGUST SEPTEMBER OCTOBER NOVEMBER DECEMBER »

- Ian Fleming, author of the James Bond spy novels, dies.

- The Lord Mayor of London calls for the pedestrianisation of the capital's Oxford, Bond and Regent main shopping streets. Almost 50 years later, the call to do the same to central London is still being made.
- The new Austin 1800, the third of Alec Issigonis's cars that follow the engineering philosophy of the Mini, is tested by Autocar. The magazine wonders if the 1800 (left) will be Issigonis's third hit in a row. It isn't, and marks the beginning of the end for BMC's product chief.
- Labour leader Harold Wilson (right) becomes PM on 16 October with a narrow majority.

- Reflective 'Luminstrip' is applied to kerbs and roundabouts in Battersea, London, as an experiment to prevent drivers hitting the sides of the road at night.

1974

THINGS HAVE NOT gone well for the UK over the previous decade. Strikes are as bad as ever as the oil crisis hit all Western Economies hard. The British Leyland group ran out of money in December 1973 and is awaiting the government's Ryder report, which will suggest possible futures for the giant company. Vauxhall and Chrysler are also on the slide.

1974 is described by Autocar staffer Jeff Daniels as a 'year of panic... when the industry was dominated by concerns over safety, emissions and the collapse of affluent markets.'

Steel prices have shot up and industry is hit by the three-day week, when energy is rationed by Edward Heath's Conservative government between January and March because of a miner's strike. Politics is on a knife-edge after two general elections fail to produce a clear majority.

■ The 'three-day week' kicks in on 1 January, restricting businesses to three days' electricity every week. TV shuts down at 10.30pm.

■ OPEC (the association of the main oil-producing nations) ends its embargo against the US, Europe and Japan after five months of cutting off supplies.

■ The 50mph speed limit on motorways is lifted.

■ The Lamborghini Countach (right) is launched. It stays on sale until 1990, though only 2042 are made.

■ Vauxhall Cross, a significant but very short section of urban motorway, opens on the south side of the Thames. But plans for a massive urban motorway scheme for the capital – on the drawing board since WW2 – are canned by the Greater London Council. Vauxhall Cross is the last section of the scheme to be built until the M11 link road in the 1990s.

■ Abba wins the Eurovision Song Contest.

JANUARY | FEBRUARY | MARCH | APRIL | MAY | JUNE

■ Autocar back on sale after a printers' strike closed the magazine. It's thought to be the first time Autocar was not on sale since it was founded.

■ New Labour chancellor Dennis Healey puts 10 per cent VAT on fuel and Autocar reports steel prices have jumped 25 per cent.

■ The Austin Allegro (left) is launched in the middle of the economic chaos, replacing the best-selling Austin 1100/1300. Autocar says 'by comparison with the Austin 1100, the Allegro offers many improvements and is in most respects a much more desirable car'.

■ PM Harold Wilson makes a statement on 25 April about struggling British Leyland. He tells the House of Commons that to let the BL group of companies fail could eventually lead to the loss of one million jobs in the UK. Although it isn't technically nationalised, the Government vows to underwrite BL's investments after banks refuse to lend the group any more money.

■ Volkswagen unveils the new Golf hatchback. Destined to remain in production for nine years, the Mk1 Golf (right) sets the pattern for the compact European hatchback that will come to dominate the new car market in future years.

■ A senior BL manager called George Turnbull resigns to work with a little-known South Korean industrial outfit called Hyundai which wants to get into car making with the Ital-designed Pony hatchback.

■ Showing the strength of dislike for the private car, London's GLC removes 8000 parking meters – 40 per cent of the total – from the capital's streets. It also closes Oxford Street to cars.

■ Citroën launches the CX (above), which replaces the iconic DS. The CX is awarded European Car of The Year for 1975 and eventually sells 1.2m units over more than a decade.

■ The first VASCAR speed camera is shown.

■ TV info service Ceefax is launched (right).

■ The Greater London Council says it wants a 'Congestion Charge'. It eventually happens 29 years later.

■ Chrysler lays off 700 people, 10 per cent of its workforce. 1750 staff are dropped by Ford.

■ During a meeting of the embattled car industry at Earls Court in London, it is revealed that UK new car sales are down 25 per cent year-on-year.

■ Japanese WW2 soldier Teruo Nakamura, who has been 'fighting' for 34 years, finally surrenders on a remote Indonesian island after the hut he is living in is spotted by a pilot flying overhead.

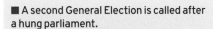

| JULY | AUGUST | SEPTEMBER | OCTOBER | NOVEMBER | DECEMBER |

■ West Germany beat the Netherlands 2-1 in the World Cup final.

■ A second General Election is called after a hung parliament.

■ General Motors Europe boss Alex Cunningham tells Autocar 'there's not enough awareness in the country of the magnitude of the problems [for the car industry]. Vauxhall made a £10m loss, he says, and 'the three day week, strikes at suppliers and shortages of steel' make for a dire situation.

■ BL's Donald Stokes (left) derides 'idle chatter around BL' predicting it will live on into the 1980s. He blames 'unrestricted imports flooding into the country' for the industry's problems.

■ The embattled industry reveals UK new car sales are down 25 per cent. The Ford Cortina 1600 XL (right) becomes the best-selling car in the UK.

1984

AFTER A DIRE four years, 1984 is a very quiet year for a poverty-stricken UK car industry as it struggles to reinvent itself.

The state of economic chaos that began in 1974 had barely let up at all during the 1970s. The Labour PM, James Callaghan, had to seek a loan from the International Monetary Fund in 1976 after a currency collapse and the UK's huge problems with strikes reached a head in the winter of 1978.

The car industry received endless blows, like much of the rest of the nationalised industry, a good portion of which also relied on government aid. Chrysler Europe collapsed in 1978 and the UK division of the manufacturer was taken over by Peugeot. A few years earlier Chrysler had managed to extract a sum of £55m from the UK government, which was used to fund the development of the Sunbeam hatchback.

Mrs Thatcher became PM in spring 1979 vowing to dismantle state aid for industry, which she thought would never stand on its own feet. Even so, she signed a cheque for £1bn to support BL, which was 'too big to fail'.

In another blow for BL – which gets renamed Austin-Rover Group during 1984 – its position as the UK's best-selling brand is usurped by Vauxhall.

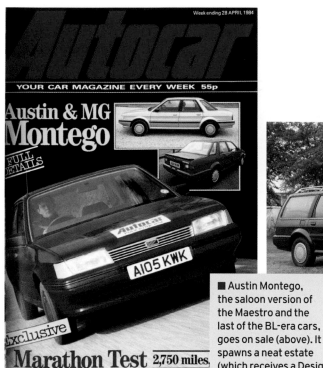

Week ending 28 APRIL 1984

Autocar

YOUR CAR MAGAZINE EVERY WEEK 55p

Austin & MG Montego FULL DETAILS

A105 KWK

Exclusive

Marathon Test 2,750 miles,

■ Austin Montego, the saloon version of the Maestro and the last of the BL-era cars, goes on sale (above). It spawns a neat estate (which receives a Design Council Award) and two MG-badged versions. However, it also suffers from build glitches.

■ The year-long miner's strike begins.

■ Legendary comedian Eric Morecambe dies.

■ The London lorry ban is back: this time the GLC wants to ban lorries at night from the capital.

JANUARY	FEBRUARY	MARCH	APRIL	MAY	JUNE

■ Despite the dismantling of state-aided industries such as steel and shipyards and rising unemployment, the UK is going through something of a revival. It is announced that new car sales in 1983 hit 1.791m, an all-time record.

■ News emerges that the government has given the green light for Jaguar to be released from BL and privatised in its own right.

■ 'Relax' by Frankie Goes to Hollywood hits No1 in the charts and shakes up the music world.

■ BL – renamed Austin-Rover Group – unveils a £5m styling studio under Roy Axe. One of the first big tasks is Project XX, a replacement for the SD1 developed with Honda, which would eventually become the Rover 800 and Honda Legend.

■ Showing unexpected creativity, ARG shows the MG Metro 6R4 Group B rally car (right). Mid-engined and all-wheel drive, it's powered by a bespoke, though troublesome, V6 turbo.

■ The Space Shuttle Discovery (below) makes its maiden flight.

■ France beat Spain 2-0 in Euro '84

■ Rumours, which eventually prove correct, suggest Honda is going to build a factory in the UK, near Swindon.

■ Wheel clamps arrive on UK roads, with London the first to get a taste of the 'Denver Boot'.

■ Vauxhall's new Mk3 Astra – with its modishly aero-influenced styling – is named European Car of the Year for 1985.

■ At the British motor show, Lotus shows the Etna concept supercar, styled by Giugiaro and powered by a V8 engine.

■ The Panther Solo sports car (left) is unveiled. Financed by a South Korean businessman, it is an MR2-style, mid-engined car powered by a 1.6-litre Ford engine. It goes through a dramatic transformation to get four-wheel drive and a Sierra Cosworth engine by the time it arrives in 1989. Fewer than 20 are thought to have been made.

■ Autocar interviews Nicholas Ridley, the Transport Minister. He says: "The last thing I want to do is persecute the motorist. I want him to be as free as possible to go where he likes, when he likes and how he likes." Ridley says he wants more parking in towns and says he believes in "competition in all areas of transport."

■ Jaguar is floated on the stock exchange. The company has looked much stronger since Sir John Egan was made chairman in 1980, reduced the workforce and made a big push on quality, especially in the important US market. Jaguar is eventually bought by Ford in 1989.

■ The radical Renault Espace MPV (above) is launched, but gets off to a slow sales start.

■ Clive Sinclair's single-seat Sinclair C5 is launched in the depths of winter. Sold as an electric vehicle, it also has pedals and exploits a loophole in the law that permits young people to ride electrically assisted bicycles on the roads.

■ The go-ahead is given for the Oxford to Birmingham section of the M40. The project attracts huge opposition from environmentalists. Although it is only 89 miles long, the M40 took from 1967 until 1990 to be completed.

JULY AUGUST SEPTEMBER OCTOBER NOVEMBER DECEMBER »

■ It's the 25th anniversary of the Mini, which has managed to stay in production, despite the 1980 Metro being intended as a replacement. Incredibly, the baby car is not killed off until 2000.

■ BL/ARG's second Honda transplant arrives in the form of the Rover 213/216 (below). It replaces the Honda Ballade-based Triumph Acclaim, which was something of a success and BL's most reliable car to date. The move marks the end of the line for the Triumph badge.

■ ARG's policy of reducing itself to just two brands continues apace. The Morris badge also reaches the end of the line, as the Ital is canned.

■ The first scoop shots of what will become the Jaguar XJ40 leak out. One of the most lengthy new car projects in memory, it eventually arrives in 1986.

■ PM Mrs Thatcher and French President François Mitterrand (right) meet about the proposed Channel Tunnel project.

■ Ford launches the Escort RS Turbo (below), an early sign that the 1980s will be the decade of the hot hatch.

1994

IT'S TWO YEARS since the Conservative party won its fourth consecutive election, and also two years after the bottom of a sharp two-year recession.

The Conservatives are fulfilling the party's long-held philosophical bent in favour of road-building by trying to push through controversial new road schemes, including the Newbury Bypass and the M11 link road, through a grid-locked East London.

The early 1990s become the time of serious anti-roads protestors – making 'Swampy' (Daniel Hooper) a household name – with thousands of like-minded activists descending on road builds in Newbury and Wanstead.

However, the Tories also promise increases in fuel duty and motorway and road pricing alongside the new roads.

The British car industry is showing strong signs of being back on its feet after recovering from near-collapse in the 1970s. New models are reviving classic brands as heritage and branding are seen as increasingly important.

German premium car makers are also poised to expand into new niches, dropping their traditional conservatism.

■ The British automotive industry is rocked by the news that BMW – then a medium-size German car maker – has bought the Rover Group from British Aerospace (which had bought it from the government in 1988) for £800m. A row ensues in the House of Commons because Rover, the last vestiges of the British-owned BL, is now in the hands of foreign owners. Honda, which had owned 20 per cent of ARG/Rover, turned down the chance to take a controlling stake.

■ Rumours emerge that BMW just wants Land Rover, and that Mini and Rover are surplus to requirements. BMW pours in billions over six years, to no great effect. Land Rover is sold to Ford and Rover/MG to a management buy-out.

■ During one of Formula 1's darkest weekends, Ayrton Senna (left) is killed in an accident during the San Marino Grand Prix. The sport is already reeling from the death of Roland Ratzenberger in a qualifying accident one day earlier, another serious accident that injures Rubens Barrichello and a start-line crash that puts a car's wheel into the crowd. Three million people line the streets for Senna's funeral in Brazil.

■ The first scoop shots of the Jaguar mule that will become the XK8 are captured. It will eventually be launched in 1996, complete with a new V8 engine, and marks an impressive leap in to the future for the company.

■ Autocar carries out the first, and only, formal road test of the McLaren F1. Built around a carbon monocoque and powered by a six-litre V12 mid-mounted engine, the F1 was finely engineered in every detail and had only a handful of bought-in components (including BMW indicator stalks and Bova coach lights).

■ Autocar reports claims that diesel pollution is 'killing' 10,000 people each year in the UK.

JANUARY FEBRUARY MARCH APRIL MAY JUNE

■ Autocar gets the scoop on what would become a landmark British car. Dubbed the 'new Lotus 7', the story reveals that a new Lotus car would get back to the company's roots by using an aluminium spaceframe to create an extremely light car. The car was the Elise (right) which was launched in 1996 to rave reviews. Weighing just 725kgs, it manages near-supercar performance from a 115bhp Rover K-series engine.

■ Autocar also gets the scoop on the new Jaguar S-type, a Ford-funded project for the company's first medium-sized executive model since the classic 1960s Mk2.

■ The Ford Mondeo (left) is European Car of the Year for 1994. Endowed with a remarkable chassis, it is a huge leap over the basic 1990 Escort.

■ The Bentley Java concept (right) is unveiled. It is another dramatic reinvention for an old British brand, showing how Vickers-owned Rolls-Royce Bentley might try to re-think the brand for the future. Insiders admit the company does not have the money needed to create the Java. Later, it turns out the Java is based on the platform of the BMW 8-series cabrio, a car that was never launched.

■ Scoop shots emerge of the all-new Mk2 Range Rover (right). It was the car that first attracted BMW to Rover (BMW supplied the diesel engine). The Germans were convinced that the luxury SUV market was set to boom, but that a BMW-badged SUV wouldn't work.

■ First flight of the Eurofighter. It doesn't go into service for another nine years.

■ The Conservative government launches the idea of road tolls, paid for by an in-car electronic smart card. The plans are announced in Cambridge, which could be the first city to take up the idea.

■ Audi launches two cars that begin the transformation of its image. It creates the original hyper-estate in the form of the Porsche-tweaked RS2 (right), which is based on the rather homely 80 wagon. It also launches the new A8 limo, which is built around a radical aluminium spaceframe.

■ Two of the most important British cars for years are launched in the same week. Land Rover's Mk2 Range Rover re-imagines the vehicle as a luxury conveyance with real off-road ability. The new X300-series Jaguar XJ is a heavy re-make of the flawed XJ40. Both cars are regarded as at least the equal of anything else. The British car industry can claim world-class ability again.

■ The massively congested section of the M25 between J10 and J15 is subject to a 50mph speed limit.

JULY   AUGUST   SEPTEMBER   OCTOBER   NOVEMBER   DECEMBER »

■ Showing his famous prescience, BMW Group's technical chief Wolfgang Reitzle predicts that all BMW cars would become 'super-frugal' after 2000. His vision was realised as Efficient Dynamics, which gave BMW a big lead when CO2 emissions became a significant factor in European Union policy.

■ Brazil beat Italy 3-2 in the World Cup.

■ The Aston Martin DB7 (below) is launched, showing another olde-worlde British brand has successfully reinvented itself.

■ At the NEC British motor show, Caterham shows the new, enclosed-wheel, 21 and TVR shows the Cerbera, which is powered by the home-grown AJP engine.

■ The new Rover 100 – aka Metro – is caught being filmed for a TV ad. It is the last car with its roots in the ill-fated BL-era still in production. The addition of a new grille and bumpers is generally thought not to be enough for the award of a Rover badge. The car still sells pretty well in the UK, though. BMW pulls production in 1998 when the 100 is crash-tested by NCAP and scores poorly.

2004

BRITAIN IS IN to the seventh year of a 13-year New Labour government. It's an administration that is far less friendly to the private motorist. Road building has been slowed to a crawl, with many projects cancelled. The emphasis is on reviving public transport and reducing car use in towns. New legislation allows road tolls to be introduced and there are new ideas such as workplace parking charges.

The British car industry has been through another shock, with the 2000 break-up and sell-off of Rover Group by BMW. MG Rover is on the brink, while Land Rover is prospering under Ford ownership. Mini, the only brand retained by BMW, is on a roll, as is Rolls-Royce, which BMW took ownership of on 1 January 2003.

■ Land Rover unveils its first-ever concept, the outlandish Range Stormer (right). It accurately predicts that the company is planning the Range Rover Sport.

■ The last Aston DB7 is built.

■ Land Rover unveils the all-new Discovery 3 (above). Its uncompromisingly brutal styling, extremely flexible seven-seat interior and all-new T5 platform shows the growing strength of the brand.

■ MG Rover shows facelifted versions of the 45 and MG ZS. The tweaked 25 and ZR in May are said to be last new models before the all-new RDX60 model arrives.

■ Autocar reports the 'threat of a £4 gallon'. The cost of fuel is still a sensitive issue after the spontaneous fuel protests of 2000 brought the country to a near standstill after four days of a fuel delivery blockade.

■ MG Rover announces that it has drawn up a new partnership with Shanghai Automotive Industry Corporation. It replaces the 2003 'deal' with China Brilliance.

JANUARY · FEBRUARY · MARCH · APRIL · MAY · JUNE

■ The Mini cabriolet (below right) is launched. It is the second car in what will become a seven-model range.

■ Facebook is launched.

■ London's controversial Congestion Charge (left) reaches its first anniversary. Although traffic in the capital is down 16 per cent, the CC massively undershoots the estimated earnings of £220m, making £65m. Plans to introduce more ambitious schemes in Edinburgh and Greater Manchester are rejected a few years later.

■ Aston Martin unveils the DB9, the first in a family of models based on the new VH aluminium platform.

■ MG Rover launches the MG SV, based on the defunct Qvale Mangusta, itself based on the De Tomaso Bigua.

■ Rolls-Royce reveals the 100EX concept (right), based on a shortened Phantom aluminium spaceframe chassis and topped with a rakish two-door, low-roof cabin.

■ Autocar reports that the explosion of 'Gatso' speed cameras and fines 'have not worked'. Despite a 40 per cent increase in speeding tickets since 2002, the number of people killed on the roads has risen by 0.6 per cent.

■ Production of the Rover V8 engine stops. Rover has been building it since 1967 and has made nearly one million units. The engine started life as the Buick 215, which was launched in 1960.

■ The Queen officially opens the massive McLaren Technology Centre in Woking.

■ A small, but vocal, movement against SUVs starts to get publicity. Government advisor David Begg wants 'higher taxes' on SUVs. London Mayor Ken Livingstone calls their drivers 'idiots' and Lib-Dem Norman Baker blames SUVs for 'school run congestion'.

■ MG Rover, despite protesting its underlying health, sells off its parts division to Caterpillar for £100m.

■ The Aston Martin DB9 Volante (above) is revealed.

■ MG Rover uses the Autocar Awards in London to reveal three new proposals based on current models: an MGF Coupé, a 75 Coupé and a high-performance MG SV-R (below).

■ A few days later MG Rover assures the press that a deal with SAIC is 'imminent' and sells the rights to the 75 and the engines and transmissions produced by its Powertrain division. In the event, the MGR production lines are halted in April 2005, and the company goes into administration with the loss of about 6000 jobs.

■ Pictures of the latest Range Rover Sport (left) are released.

JULY AUGUST SEPTEMBER OCTOBER NOVEMBER DECEMBER ≫

■ It's revealed that TVR has been sold to a Russian investor called Nikolay Smolensky for a rumoured £15m.

■ Scoop shots of MG Rover's proposed RDX60 range leak out – the unusual styling confounds many observers. MG Rover also claims it will be profitable by 'the end of 2005'.

■ The 500,000th BMW Mini (right) since launch in mid-2001 is made at the company's Oxford factory.

■ Land Rover's Solihull plant is read the riot act by Ford boss Mark Fields, who demands "big improvements in quality and productivity".

■ Jaguar announces it will close the historic Browns Lane site in 2005. The company has been there since 1951.

SIXY

It may not be a hypercar, but the Mercedes G63 AMG 6x6 is as exotic and attention-grabbing as the best of them. **Greg Kable** drives it in Dubai

Despite its weight, G63 can get all six wheels off the deck

Somewhere in the middle of a vast desert, my passenger, Mercedes-Benz G-class development boss Axel Harries, and I start to laugh hysterically. I have just dropped the hulking great G63 AMG 6x6 down a couple of gears and nailed it in a bid to gain enough momentum to clear a massive wall of sand. Scrambling across the soft surface, the engine unleashes a baritone blare through a quartet of side pipes that exits beneath the rear doors as we're fired up the long, sandy ascent. As we approach the summit, the nose of the big Benz tilts skywards and we're propelled over the top of the dune – all six wheels off the ground.

Coming to a standstill in a cloud of dust on the other side, Harries turns to me and, holding back a smile, suggests that we should do it again, but with added run-up. It's enough to send me into a fit of laughter at the sheer capability of what is surely the most outrageous Mercedes-Benz road car ever to wear a licence plate.

This is motoring, Dubai style. The United Arab Emirates may be relatively small, but with some 29,000 square miles of desert out of a total of 32,000 square miles of land mass, it's a place where big off-roaders rule. With vast amounts of oil wealth, Emiratis regularly splurge on modified off-roaders, not so much to signal their riches but

BEAST

Mercedes-Benz G63 AMG 6x6

Price	£350,000 (est)
0-62mph	Under 6.0sec
Top speed	100mph (limited)
Economy	15.0mpg (est)
CO₂	na
Kerb weight	3775kg
Engine	V8, 5461cc, twin-turbo, petrol
Installation	Front, longitudinal, 6WD
Power	536bhp at 5500rpm
Torque	560lb ft at 2000rpm
Gearbox	7-spd automatic
Length	5875mm
Width	2110mm
Height	2210mm
Wheelbase	4220mm (front to rear axle)
Tracks f/r	1790mm
Ground clearance	460mm
Fording depth	1000mm
Max approach angle	52deg
Max departure angle	54deg
Breakover angle	22deg
Payload	650kg
Fuel tank	159 litres
Wheels	12.5Jx37in (inc tyres)
	ProComp Xtreme

simply because they can. Still, there's only so much that an oil-rich sheikh can do to a Range Rover, Porsche Cayenne or BMW X6, which is where this latest and more extreme take on the venerable G-class comes in.

Set to be produced alongside standard versions of the 34-year-old off-roader from late this year, the G63 6x6 has been conceived as the ultimate money-no-object off-roader, with a 5.5-litre V8, six driven wheels, genuine low-range gearing, five differential locks and on-board compressors for a tyre control system that allows you to quickly alter pressures to suit the prevailing conditions.

The colossal pick-up started life as an even more rugged military version of the G320 CDI, originally engineered for the Australian army and in operation since 2011. Harries suggests that, at about £350,000, the G63 6x6 will be Mercedes' second most expensive model after the new SLS Electric Drive.

Unlike the military-spec G320 CDI 6x6, the G63 gets a twin-turbocharged AMG V8 with 536bhp. Torque is a not insignificant 560lb ft and is crucial in providing the shove required to haul the big 6x6's 3775kg kerb weight.

Another significant feature is Mercedes' 7G-tronic seven-speed automatic transmission, which incorporates a transfer case capable of

The driving position is old-school but the cabin is up-to-date

← altering between a 0.87:1 high-range ratio for on-road driving and 2.16:1 low-range for off-road use, to all six wheels in a nominal 30/40/30 split. And, just for good measure, there are no fewer than five electronic differential locks, offering 100 per cent lock-up of all six wheels.

Massive 37-inch wheels feature a bead-plate design that allows their 12.5-inch-wide tyres to be inflated and deflated at will from a switch sited in the headlining.

At 5875mm long, 2110mm wide and 2210mm tall, the G63 6x6 is 1106mm longer, 225mm wider and 272mm taller than the standard 4x4 version. Along with a 300mm increase in the wheelbase through to the middle axle, at 3120mm, the front and middle axles have also increased in width by 281mm each, at 1790mm.

Ground clearance is a whopping 460mm. The approach angle has been increased by 16deg to 52deg and the departure angle is now 54kg, a rise of 27deg. The breakover angle has also increased, by 1deg, to 22deg.

Despite all of its pretensions, the maximum payload capacity in the polished bamboo-trimmed tray bed at the back is a somewhat disappointing 650kg. Structural strengthening, meanwhile, is provided by a substantial stainless steel roll cage.

The early prototype that we drove was terrifically well engineered and the big surprise is just how well refined it is, both mechanically and in terms of how it goes, stops and handles.

I'm not sure how it would fare running down the local high street on the school run, but there's no doubt that you'd be noticed. And, really, that's what

this new Mercedes-Benz is all about. Once you've heaved yourself way up on to the substantial step plate and into the heavily contoured sports seat, you discover an interior that, apart from the height, is little changed in look, character and quality from that of the standard G63.

The upright driving position is decidedly old-school, as is the near-vertical windscreen and shallow dashboard, but it all affords brilliant forward vision, with the indicators mounted atop the front wings acting as positioning points. Less well resolved, however, is the rear view, which is hampered by the tall rear seatbacks and a small two-piece rear window.

The 300mm increase in wheelbase length through to the middle axle provides the basis for a longer cabin than the existing G63's.

Harries indicates that the production version will be capable of running from a standstill to 62mph in less than 6.0sec

Reflecting the vehicle's luxury billing, there's a liberal covering of Alcantara, and the standard three-across rear bench seat is replaced by two individual leather-lined and electrically adjustable AMG sports seats.

The exhausts' engaging blare lends the monstrous Mercedes an eager demeanour as you hit the starter but, once under way, the G63 6x6 proves remarkably easy to drive. It may have been conceived for army duties in the outback, but the work focused on converting it for civilian use has provided it with a straightforward nature and a level of comfort that you'd hardly credit.

In the dunes of Dubai's desert, the G63 6x6 feels as invincible as its looks. Those big tyres work in concert with the complex driveline to provide plenty of traction, allowing you to accelerate from a standstill with urgency and cruise at highway speeds on sandy tracks without any great trepidation. Meanwhile, steep dunes and daunting sinkholes are taken in its stride.

Mercedes hasn't quoted official acceleration times, but Harries indicates that the production version will be capable of running from a standstill to 62mph in less than six seconds, which is nothing short of amazing. Top speed, limited by those balloon-like tyres, is governed to 100mph, although there could be scope to raise it slightly with more road-biased rubber.

Given room to move, the G63 6x6 provides surprising stability, helped by its longer wheelbase and two extra wheels. The ride is also far less choppy than that of the 4x4 G63, with a noticeable reduction in sharp vertical movements.

With such height, there is a good deal of lean in corners, but the body movement is wonderfully progressive and superbly controlled. The adoption of an Öhlins damper system and massive springs also provides great comfort, and when the conditions become really tough the excellent wheel articulation and multitude of diff lock combinations ensure that all six wheels are firmly planted for impressive progress.

It's unlikely that any sheikh will be concerned about fuel consumption, but we asked anyway. Unofficially, we're told, it will be in the region of 15mpg on the combined cycle. Just as well, then, that the production G63 6x6 will come with two fuel tanks with an overall capacity of 159 litres.

You could argue long and hard about the merits or otherwise of the Mercedes-Benz AMG G63 6x6. However, it is deeply satisfying to drive and hugely capable in the most extreme conditions.

Right now, Mercedes is looking at an annual run of between 20 and 30 examples of the G63 6x6 per year, but if the interest it stirred during our time with it in the UAE is any indication, that's not going to be enough.

Not if members of the Dubai royal family and their friends, who showed up as we were photographing it in the desert and demanded an on-the-spot test drive, get their way. And I'm sure that they will. A

The three-seat rear bench is replaced by two individual chairs

Those who are weak, small or get vertigo may well struggle

WORTH THE WAIT

So does Jaguar's first sports car since the E-type live up to the hype? We drive all three variants

PHOTOGRAPHY STAN PAPIOR

THE JAGUAR F-TYPE, one of the most significant cars to be launched this year, is the sportiest Jaguar since the XJ220. And the F really *is* a sports car, they've told me, at some length. It ain't like any other Jaguar, they say. You'll notice "within 50 metres, not 50km", says Ian Hoban, the F-type's line manager.

What makes it so different from a 'normal' Jaguar, then? There's nothing much wrong with one of those, I thought. The F-type, like the XK, is built from aluminium alloys, and both are front-engined, rear-wheel-drive roadsters. But the F-type's shell is 30 per cent stiffer, torsionally, than an XK's. It's shorter by a foot, wider by a thumb width and lower by 120mm – as sits its driver.

Among its rivals, Jaguar counts not the Mercedes-Benz SL but the Porsche 911 cabriolet, Audi R8 Spyder and Aston V8 Vantage roadster. Only, Jaguar says, the F is about 25 per cent cheaper than those. It has a graph to prove it. A graph on which Porsche's Boxster, mind you, is notable by its absence at a lower price still.

But anyway it looks like Jaguar has indeed identified a position, a little gap, between the Boxster and 911 where, frankly, I didn't think one existed. No F-type variant epitomises that identity more than our test car – this mid-table 3.0-litre supercharged V6 S in white, bringing with it 375 old British brake horsepower and 339lb ft of torque.

Like all F-types, the V6 S's motor is longitudinally mounted at the front and mated to an eight-speed ZF automatic transmission. Not a dual-clutch auto, mind, but a traditional slusher – although a torque converter which locks up so early that it spends all its time above crawling speed directly linked to the rear wheels, ensuring that it's slush-free. What's unlike other F-types is that the V6 S gets a conventional mechanical limited-slip differential. The base V6 does without a locking diff and the V8 S has an electronic locking one. The 15kg weight penalty that the V8's 'e-diff' brings would spoil what Jaguar claims is 50/50 weight distribution. It also claims 0-60mph in 4.8sec and a top speed of 171mph for this version, which sounds plenty quick enough to me. The price is £67,520, which sounds plenty, too.

All in all, though, it's a reassuringly heady, old-school, burly mechanical set-up whose promise is further enhanced by double wishbones all round and hydraulic, rather than electric, assistance for the power steering, and to hell with the economy and emissions (which, for the record, are 31.0mpg and 213g/km for the V6 S). The last time Jaguar launched a car like this, though, its steering was unassisted. Think E-type, or perhaps

A V6 S brings with it 375 old British brake horsepower

The fluid, precise steering response is one of the F-type's delights, but there are plenty of others, including eager performance

The driver sits lower than in, say, an XK and the whole design is focused on his or her needs; Jaguar calls the cabin layout a '1+1'

Austin-Healey, Triumph TR6, maybe even TVR. That's the kind of vibe the F-type emanates.

Except, of course, it combines all that with a touch of 21st century luxury. This is a well appointed and well trimmed car, with an interesting cabin and some pleasing materials and neat touches. I could live without the rising centre air vents (they only pop out when there's more serious cooling or heating to be done) if it meant I could have higher-quality-feel gearshift paddles on the wheel, but generally, you have to admit, it's a pretty well finished cockpit. It's not that sensible, though – hey, it's a sports car, guv'nor – and Jaguar calls the F-type a '1+1' because of the way that the cockpit's feel is divided into two, with the driver getting more 'technical' surfaces. But the truth is →

Switch by the gear selector adjusts driving modes; boot is a modest 201 litres; deflector cuts buffeting, but it's still breezy in cabin

On such roads, the F-type flows through the bends

This Jaguar is something different. And yes, special

← that if you wanted to carry anything more than a couple of squashy bags, you'd end up using the passenger space, too. This isn't a terribly practical car. It may be cheaper than a 911, but that has '+2' rear seats, and their benefit isn't negligible.

The F-type feels suitably *sportif*. The driving position is straight and low, with pedals set up so that left or right-foot braking are both easy. The steering wheel is widely adjustable (although I wouldn't mind it coming closer to the driver) and, with the equipment fitted to our test car, has a heated leather rim. I quite like that. It's only about 10deg in northern Spain as we continue on some terrific roads and the F-type, roof down, is a touch blustery. Not unacceptably so, but definitely it's more sports car in here than tousle-free grand tourer.

Still, so far I've discovered that the ride is pretty good – at least, as far as I can tell on these roads, lacking the harshness and brittleness of some of Wales's worst as they do, but that's to be expected. They're smooth enough that you can use – all the time – the F-type's Dynamic mode, which brings firmer calibration to the dampers, tightening body control, as well as adding weight to the steering and sharpening the throttle and gearbox response.

And it's that steering which, when we first headed out on to the roads a few hours ago, was the first indication that this Jaguar is something different. And yes, something special.

It's true: I noticed it within 50m (50cm, probably). The steering retains the oiliness and slickness that's traditional with a Jaguar rack, but it has the quickest ratio ever fitted to a Jaguar. It isn't hyperactive, at 2.5 turns lock to lock, but it gives the 1614kg roadster a sense of immediacy and purpose. And on our drive to this point, I've enjoyed that. It is different from other Jaguars, and in no bad way. The underlying DNA is still there, it seems to me, in that loping ride and the smoothness of the gearbox, but it has been stretched outwards. From this moment, a Jaguar can stand for something different.

Nothing displays that quite like the V6 S's engine, I think. There are some terrific roads around here: quiet, wide, hilly. It's the sort of place where you can accelerate for a few seconds and then back off again, between the numerous hairpins.

The V6 isn't the smoothest motor on the block; it revs to about 7000rpm and makes its peak output at 6500rpm, but I haven't run into the limiter by mistake, and nor am I likely to. Because it's supercharged, the response is true and immediate, but if you're looking for a sonorous, high-revving unit, a Porsche is the place. There's character enough at lower revs, though. With the S's active exhaust bypass valves in their angry position, there are some real fireworks on the overrun. I promise this is the best description I can give you: you know the snare drum bits from the theme tune to *Where Eagles Dare*? It sounds like those. Just like those. Time it right and you can hum the theme tune and intersperse it with drum rolls. Not that photographer Papior and I did that. No, no, no.

Electrically operated roof can be raised or lowered in 12 seconds at speeds of up to 30mph; its fabric layers include a Thinsulate lining to keep unwanted cold and noise at bay

It feels beautifully straight and secure at speed

It's 4470mm long, just 21mm shorter than a Porsche 911

Mike Cross, Jaguar's chief engineer for vehicle integrity, smiles when he's asked about it. "It's what cars naturally do," he says. "Our engineers have to work incredibly hard to take that sort of noise out." And here they are, asking them to leave them in.

So far, then, so impressive. So why my hesitancy about this car? One: it's no more practical than a Boxster but looks, at its base price, quite a lot lumpier. Two: it rides; it glides. It's an excellent motorway companion, in fact, running beautifully straight and secure at speed. But sometimes, on twistier roads, I think I fear the body control is a little loose; this is a heavier car than some of those around it, and loose body movements are hard to keep in check without nailing

the ride down. Our photographic demands mean that we've missed our opportunity to drive it on the track. But I'm just waiting for that bit of road to really prove the F's credentials as a sports car.

Photography, inevitably, provides it. There's an uphill stretch of road that starts off lined by green, lush fields, and as it rises the green gives way to rocky outcrops. At the top, vultures circle on thermals and, halfway along, Papior spots the ideal corner. It will take several runs before the shot is in the bag. Turning points are a few corners away, each side, of the one he wants to use.

It's as ideal a piece of proving road as you'll find for a sporting roadster. And by gum, actually, this car gets →

Supercharged 3.0-litre V6 delivers 375bhp, 339lb ft and fireworks on the overrun

F-TYPE V6: THE STARTER MODEL DRIVEN

There's a delicacy to the way the entry-level V6 F-type drives that not even the delightful V6 S can replicate in certain circumstances. Its steering seems especially sweet, as does its ride, both of which are almost certainly the result of it rolling on smaller, visually less arresting 18-inch wheels, which also happen to bring slightly higher-profile and therefore slightly more comfortable 18-inch Pirelli P Zero tyres.

It flows beautifully along any road, the V6, feeling nimbler but also a lot less manic than the He-Man V8 S. Yet it's still perfectly quick enough, with 0-60mph taking just 5.2sec. That's the sort of thrust that impresses rather than frightens. For many of Jaguar's new customers (as many as 85 per cent of F-type buyers will be new to the brand), the V6 might well be the perfect cocktail of grip, grunt, style and desirability.

And for the purist, it might even provide the most satisfying driving experience of the three models. How so? Because you can drive the V6 hard on the road without scaring yourself, or incurring the wrath of other road users, which is a genuine concern in the V8 S. Its handling balance might also be the sweetest of

the range, with almost no understeer to speak of on the road, and no oversteer, either, because there isn't the torque to unearth the rear tyres like there is in the other models.

The gearbox also works especially well in the V6, again because it doesn't have such a big hit of torque to deal with. Indeed, Jaguar's new Quickshift eight-speed transmission feels more like a DSG in the V6 than it does in either of the other models.

What you don't get in the V6, you might not miss anyway. There's no limited-slip diff, and no Dynamic Drive system that allows you to fiddle with the engine, gearbox, damper or throttle settings. What you get is a traditional rear-drive sports car, pure and simple. With emphasis on the pure rather than on the simple.
STEVE SUTCLIFFE

It has fine balance and is still quick: 0-60mph in 5.2sec

F-TYPE V8 S: THE UNHINGED OPTION DRIVEN

There's a monumental step up in performance when you climb out of a V6 F-type – either of them – and ensconce yourself in the V8 S. The noise that it makes is totally different, for starters. The response from its power steering is also meatier – a lot meatier. Even its bodyshell shimmies slightly when you press the throttle, like those of all the finest hot rods do.

But it's what happens when you put your foot down in the V8 F-type, preferably with a lowish gear engaged within the new eight-speed Quickshift gearbox and ideally on a quiet and straight ribbon of road, that distinguishes this car as The Superior Being. The way that it accelerates is, frankly, brutal and maybe even a little

It's the choice for adenalin junkies and drift seekers

bit scary to begin with – to a point where I genuinely believe that some customers might find it a touch too much. In which case, they will need to go away and learn their craft behind the wheel of a V6 instead.

For the truly unhinged enthusiast, though, the V8 S is the only F-type to have. Jaguar reckons that it'll do zero to 100mph in 8.9sec, which is deeply quick. But the way that this British sports car thunders towards the horizon at the merest prod of the throttle in any of the first five gears makes it feel quicker, even, than such a number would suggest.

The response from its 5.0-litre V8 is fantastic. If you didn't know it was supercharged, you'd never guess. But it's the way the acceleration keeps on coming at you that makes the V8 seem so seductive, so addictive, so much more appealing at its core than either of the merely fast V6s.

The way that the gearbox picks off gears so efficiently when you short-shift up the ratios is fairly delicious, too, as is the amount of traction on offer with the new e-diff switched to Normal. (Massive, lairy tail slides can

Sutcliffe calls the V8 F-type addictive

also be delivered at will if you then decide to switch it off.)

As for the sound it makes, it is epic: a deep rumble below 2000rpm that rises through a satanic roar between there and 4500rpm, finishing in a very loud, very lovely scream between 5000rpm and the red line.

It's the sort of car that you climb out of after a decent thrash across a good road, glad still to be in one piece, heart thumping, mind fizzing with

adrenalin. It reminds me of the most sorted TVR that there ever was, and I mean that entirely as a compliment.

It won't appeal to everyone as such (although initial orders suggest that the V8 S is accounting for some 40 per cent of overall interest), but to those who want the biggest bang possible from their latest sports car, the V8 S F-type has few equals. Virtually at any price.
STEVE SUTCLIFFE

Price of the V6 S is a cool £67,520, before options

When provoked, the F-type will provide more oversteer

V6 S is capable of 0-62mph in 4.8sec and 171mph

JAGUAR F-TYPE V6 S

Price	£67,520
0-62mph	4.8sec
Top speed	171mph (limited)
Economy	31.0mpg
CO_2 emissions	213g/km
Kerb weight	1614kg
Engine layout	V6, 2995cc, supercharged, petrol
Power	375bhp at 6500rpm
Torque	339lb ft at 3500-5000rpm
Power to weight	232bhp per tonne
Specific output	125bhp per litre
Compression ratio	10.5:1
Gearbox	8-spd automatic
Length	4470mm
Width	1923mm
Height	1296mm
Wheelbase	2622mm
Fuel tank	72 litres
Range	490 miles
Boot	201 litres
Front suspension	Double wishbones, coil springs, anti-roll bar
Rear suspension	Double wishbones, coil springs, anti-roll bar
Brakes	380mm ventilated discs (f), 376mm ventilated discs (r)
Wheels	9.0Jx20in (f), 10.5Jx20in (r)
Tyres	255/35 ZR20 (f), 295/30 ZR30 (r)

← it right. There is a touch of slack in the body movements over crests, as I suspected, but it's not unacceptable. It's predictable, slight, manageable. Top-spec Mercedes SLKs and BMW Z4s? Forget 'em. They don't have anything like the capacity in their ride as this car.

The steering is incisive, and there's a touch of road feel. It's not loaded with it, but there's enough. The brakes feel a little over-servoed at the very top of their travel, but afterwards they are very progressive. And the balance is spot on. There's a touch of understeer on the way in and a touch of oversteer on the way out. Turning the stability control off is one prolonged poke of the switch away and, when provoked, the F-type will provide yet more oversteer on demand.

Jaguar says this car "isn't a drift machine", but at heart, that part of its DNA which is common to all Jaguars is still there: the long wheelbase, the decent balance, and a group of engineers who sometimes just really like doing that sort of thing.

I know that it can seem a bit daft, but when chassis engineers take the

time to ensure that a car goes into and comes out of a slide with the elegance of this – Lotus's engineers take the time, too – it says good things about their whole approach to dynamics. Every detail is nailed, and the car is better as a result.

It is better, too. Better than I'd credited before some reflection. In

some ways the F-type is a simple roadster, but there's genuine dynamic ability beneath it.

Which is just as well, given where Jaguar has priced it. In its base form, the F-type costs £10,000 more than the equivalent Z4 before you get jiggy with options on either. That means you have to part with £67,520 to step into a V6 S. Further up the F-type range, where the meatier V8 S lives, it's less of an issue, but there's no question that this new Jaguar sports car is priced with confidence.

Justifiably? I think so. In fact, I think there is only one manufacturer that Jaguar has to worry about when it comes to the F-type. Trouble is, it's from Stuttgart, and it makes not one but two compelling models...

MATT PRIOR

Design details have been worked to keep the surfaces looking as clean as possible

F-TYPE vs 911, BOXSTER
Porsche had to summon all of its firepower to take on the new Jaguar, the most talked about sports car of the year

AUTOCAR'S GREATEST IMAGES
A selection of our favourite pictures from the lenses of our expert photographers

PHOTOGRAPHY STAN PAPIOR, STUART PRICE, JED LEICESTER, PETER SPINNEY, MALCOLM GRIFFITHS

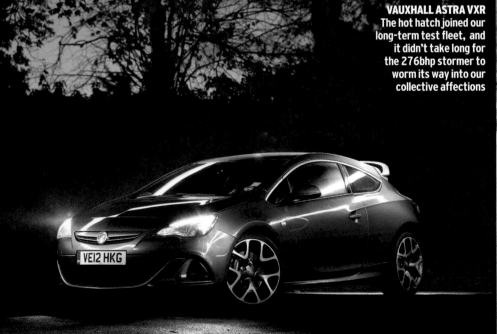

VAUXHALL ASTRA VXR
The hot hatch joined our long-term test fleet, and it didn't take long for the 276bhp stormer to worm its way into our collective affections

THREE-WAY DRAG RACE
You know we have too much time on our hands when we dream up a race between a rallycross racer, a BMW superbike and an Ariel Atom

BACK TO THE START
To celebrate 100 years of car production in Oxford, Hilton Holloway hitched a ride in what is believed to be the first Morris-Oxford 10hp car

SNOW BUSINESS
Richard Bremner put Volvo's advanced new V60 Plug-In Hybrid through its paces by driving it across the frozen, snow-clad expanses of Sweden

HANDLE WITH FLAIR
A mouthwatering array of performance cars are assembled for Autocar's annual Handling Day contest. In this shot, an Alpina B3 GT3 and Lotus Exige S hassle Merc's C63 AMG Black Series

STILL FEISTY AT FORTY
Caterham celebrated
four decades of building
the famous Seven in
2013. Andrew Frankel
compared an early
example against its
modern equivalent to
assess what's changed
through the years

FLY LIKE AN EAGLE
If you lust after a Jaguar
E-type and have £600k
to spare, Eagle in East
Sussex will build you a
modern reinterpretation
of the icon. Then you can
have fun doing this...

NEW CARS THAT STIRRED OUR SOULS THIS YEAR

OVER THE NEXT two-dozen pages, we bring you a selection of the most interesting, exciting and significant new car launches attended by Autocar's testers this year.

To describe the vehicles featured herein as a 'mixed bag' would be an understatement; 2013 was another captivating year when it came to new cars, with a blend of unhinged supercars, practical crossovers, sensible city runabouts and cutting-edge hybrids all making the headlines.

If a theme underpins the cars we've highlighted from nearly 200 reviews written by our experts, it is that the standard of cars gets nudged ever higher with each passing year.

In 2013, prospective buyers had more choice than ever across almost every market segment. With car makers diversifying model ranges and downsizing engines, customers have rarely had a greater range of options and derivatives to choose from.

IN THIS SECTION

70

76

86

88

Lamborghini
Aventador Roadster

The famous Italian manufacturer celebrates 50 years of creating outrageous sports cars with the drop-top Aventador, which promises wind-in-your-hair motoring at no less than 217mph

The seats, wheel, dashboard and instrument binnacle are all shared with the coupé

THE AVENTADOR ROADSTER is the most extraordinary Lamborghini in the company's illustrous 50-year history. Or so claimed Lamborghini's charismatic chairman, Stephan Winkelmann, at the car's launch in Miami earlier this year.

It's a bold claim, given what has been served up previously by the famous old supercar maker from Sant'Agata – the Miura SV and pretty much any version of the Countach are surely contenders. Then again, one look at the mighty Aventador Roadster in the flesh tells you that it is indeed right up there with Lamborghini's most outrageous creations. It looks like the sort of car Batman might drive on his day off, maybe when he's on holiday in Miami Beach...

Don't think of the Roadster as some kind of folly, however, or as a car that hasn't somehow been engineered thoroughly for the job. Unlike the Murciélago Roadster, which was something of an after-thought to be honest, the open-top Aventador is a stand-alone model in its own right.

The styling is unique, and considerable care and attention have been employed to ensure that it has a separate, more extrovert personality than the coupé. Although it shares its basic carbonfibre tub platform, 6.5-litre V12 engine and seven-speed single-clutch gearbox with the coupé, subtle changes under the skin mean it is perhaps more impressive dynamically than the fixed-head – for reasons we'll come to in a moment.

Despite weighing some 50kg more than the coupé, the Roadster is said by Lamborghini to be capable of setting exactly the same time around the number one handling circuit at the Nardo test facility in the hands of its main test drivers. Had the roof simply been removed and various areas of the car not been redesigned to compensate for the decrease in fundamental stiffness, there is no way that the Roadster could achieve such raw speed across the ground.

And on the road that's exactly how it feels: pure, fast and sharp and perhaps a touch more precise than →

The V12 puts out 700bhp at 8250rpm and has the timbre and volume to stir the soul

Overall, the Roadster just feels grippier than the coupé everywhere and at least as well balanced

←the coupé at the front end thanks to the fitment of bigger-diameter tyres (optional 21-inch 355/25s at the back with 20-inch 255/35s at the front on our test car). These, say Lamborghini's testers, make a small but key difference to front-end bite during the turn-in phase.

The result is a less understeery car in slow corners (which is welcome) without there being any extra nervousness at the back in fast corners (ditto). Overall, the Roadster just feels grippier than the coupé everywhere, and at least as well balanced near its monumental limits.

So although it might weigh an extra 50kg, the Roadster gives little, if anything, away to the coupé from behind the wheel. Other than the fact that there's no roof, it even feels the same when you're in the driving seat, which is no surprise given that the dashboard, instruments, switchgear and seats are all identical to those of the fixed-head car.

The roof itself comes in two forged carbon panels that are removed by unlocking a couple of latches and lifting them out manually. Each panel weighs just 3kg and stores neatly beneath the bonnet in the boot.

Once in situ, they render the luggage capacity all but useless but then, as Lamborghini says, "You don't buy a car like this to go shopping with". Which is fair enough, even if it would be handy to be able to put something slightly larger than a toothbrush in the boot when the sun comes out.

Rather more impressive (and entirely believable) is Lamborghini's claim that the Roadster can reach its astonishing 217mph top speed with or without the roof in place. The highest speed I reached was about 160mph along the main straight at the Homestead-Miami Speedway, at

which point any noise generated by the wind was drowned out completely by the machinations of that monster V12.

At lower speeds, however, it's clear that Lamborghini's designers and aerodynamicists have done a fine job of managing the flow of air away from the cockpit. At 80mph with the windows up and the small rear bulkhead screen raised, conversation is easy to maintain. Unlike the Murciélago Roadster, there's a true level of refinement to this car's demeanour when you're driving it al fresco, up to and beyond three figures.

But the best way to drive it is with

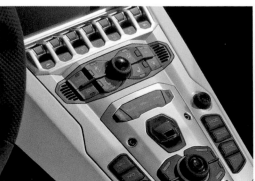

The tyre mix of 255/30 ZR20 front and 355/25 ZR21 rear improves front-end bite; that needle will run all the way to 8500rpm; the cabin styling is unmistakably Lamborghini

The Roadster never feels athletic but it grips better and turns in smarter than the coupé

Eco-tech arrives at Lamborghini

THE AVENTADOR IS far from the greenest car on the planet, but most owners couldn't care less about fuel consumption and emissions. However, Lamborghini has made significant strides to improve the eco credentials of its flagship car for the 2013 model year, hence the reason there is now a capacitor-based stop-start system, a much more efficient recharging process for the battery and a cylinder-deactivation set-up that operates below 84mph and on light throttle loads. All of this has improved the economy and CO_2 emission by up to 25 per cent overall. That's an admirable achievement, even if the official emissions figure remains at a somewhat scary 370g/km, with a combined consumption of just 17.5mpg.

the roof up and the bulkhead panel that sits behind your head down. This tiny glass panel is the only thing that separates your ears and brain from the screaming, 700bhp V12, and when you lower it, the volume levels become cataclysmically intense. You can smell the unleaded being burned, and it sounds far, far angrier – and simply louder – than the coupé does at any stage within the 8500rpm rev range. At times you'll be wondering if it might actually be doing permanent damage to your ears.

Faults? The ride is skateboard stiff

Lambo's roof comprises two folding panels

on the public road and the steering weights up too quickly and too much in fast corners. And despite the excellence of the transformation from coupé to Roadster, the Aventador still feels like a big, heavy and almost clumsy machine if and when you start to throw it around. But, fundamentally, it is what it is and you'll either love it or hate it for that.

Times may be hard for the mainstream car manufacturers at the moment, but for the likes of Lamborghini, the opposite is true in 2013, and it's the Asian market that's

keeping trade strong. Hence the reason why, even at £288,840, the Roadster is sold out until mid-way through 2014.

It is indeed a crazy kind of world in which a nigh-on £300,000 Roadster can outsell Lotus's entire line-up in one year by a factor of three. But then the Aventador Roadster is a crazy kind of car. Despite it being one of the more ostentatious examples of how the chasm between the haves and the have-nots has widened, it's also a wondrous machine in its own right.

It's a flawed diamond of a car that does things in its own inimitable way, and forget what the rest of us might think in the process. A proper way to Lambo to celebrate its 50th birthday, in other words.

STEVE SUTCLIFFE

LAMBORGHINI AVENTADOR LP 700-4 ROADSTER

Price	£288,840
0-62mph	3.0sec
Top speed	217mph
Economy	17.5mpg (combined)
CO2	370g/km
Kerb weight	1625kg (dry)
Engine	V12, 6498cc, petrol
Installation	Mid, longitudinal, four-wheel drive
Power	700bhp at 8250rpm
Torque	509lb ft at 5500rpm
Gearbox	7-spd auto
Fuel tank	90 litres
Boot	na
Wheels	9Jx20in (f), 13Jx21in (r)
Tyres	255/30 ZR20 (f), 355/25 ZR21 (r)

MANUFACTURER'S CLAIMED FIGURES

Ford Fiesta ST

Warm ST badge returns to Ford's supermini after a five-year absence, aiming to provide a fast, fun package that can be driven every day

THIS IS THE latest fast Ford, then. The first hot Fiesta that'll be sold globally, and the first production Fiesta to reach 62mph from rest in under seven seconds, it says here, which sounds particularly sprightly.

As well it might: it has 179bhp, which, although around 10 per cent less than the class's fastest, should prove sufficient in a four-metre supermini that weighs 1163kg.

That output – strong but not outstanding – gives you an idea of where Ford wants the Fiesta ST to sit.

Unlike Renault or Peugeot, Ford doesn't have one sporting line. It has both ST and RS badges to use, giving the flexibility to let STs be daily drivers and RSs hardcore models.

Power comes from a turbocharged 1.6-litre Ecoboost four-pot that drives the front wheels through a six-speed manual gearbox. There's no flappy paddle option, and neither is there a mechanical limited-slip diff – the preserve of RS models, you feel. Instead, the Fiesta gets Torque Vectoring Control, an extension of stability control that brakes a spinning inside wheel, replicating some of an LSD's work. The suspension is 15mm lower than on regular Fiestas, and spring and damper rates are appropriately a mite stiffer, as is the rear torsion beam.

What else? The power steering is electrically assisted and uses a different, faster (2.4 turns) rack, although it remains linear; unlike a Servotronic system, it doesn't get faster as you wind on more lock to increase agility.

To the cabin. Around it are dotted a few highlights that mark the Fiesta out from the cooking models. Nothing you wouldn't expect, mind, just a few jewelled highlights, including a pleasingly sculpted (and round) steering wheel.

The driving position is pretty good, but not ideal for yours truly. I found the seat squab too angled if you set it low, giving too much beef under the thigh, while the steering wheel

doesn't stretch quite close enough for me. Best to sit a little higher with a more upright seatback for easy wheel twiddling, I found. But it's a small niggle; you can get comfy enough.

Mechanical detail, then. There's a push-button starter on this ST-2, and the motor fires to a quiet idle. The clutch and throttle actions and gearshift are slick too. Ford apportions its control weights well, and the ST is no exception. There's a tiny amount of mechanical resistance on the gearshift but it's very precise and easy, and throttle response is good, with little appreciable lag at low revs.

On motorway surfaces, the ride immediately feels firm but well damped. There's a reasonable amount of vertical movement, but the ST doesn't react harshly to the bumps that cause it. Yet it retains tight control of its body as a result of the tautness. Instantly it feels good. It's

The cabin isn't complemented by the best driving position, but it is comfy enough

Rear's better for two, but it will take three

ST feels agile and responsive when pushed

quick enough, too. The official claim is 6.9sec to 62mph, and that feels about right to me. Swapping cogs is easy and the engine revs with some enthusiasm to the 6500rpm redline, with responses that improve higher in the rev range (although, as with most turbo petrol units, it's not really worth revving out the last few hundred revs).

Thanks to a sound symposer (see sidebar, right), the 1.6 Ecoboost sounds pretty good, too – not five-pot-replicating like that of the bigger Focus ST, but powerful and smooth nonetheless, yet quiet enough on a tickled throttle that a motorway cruise is easy and quiet. It's a good match for the car's fine stability and sufficient comfort.

The Fiesta steers well, too. It's slick and oily, with a decent simulation of the weighting you'd get from a hydraulic system: a gradual build-up of resistance, as if you're beginning to ease lateral pressure onto the tyres. You're not *really* feeling it, mind; electrically assisted systems, improving daily though they are, are still less communicative than the best hydraulic set-ups. It's a bit like listening to a digital piano rather than a real one: so clean and consistent that you can sense it's a replicant. Still, it's better than an even half-decent hydraulic rack. Let's not kid ourselves, car makers can turn out good and bad steering systems regardless of the hardware, and Ford does them well.

And if you're pushing on? The Fiesta ST is happy to be pushing on with you. It turns with agility and showed good traction even out of tight second-gear corners in damp testing conditions. Across challenging cambers and crests, even if they arrive mid-corner, the Fiesta's body control is terrific and the chassis is composed and controllable. It's not as keenly focused as the recently departed Renault Clio 200 Cup, but it isn't really meant to be.

Eventually the Fiesta will push wide at the front on a steady throttle, and in the dry it will apparently lift a rear wheel. Not in the damp, mind, but with some provocation (more than the Renault would ask) it's happy to oversteer controllably on the way into a corner. The stability control has three modes: on, sport (which will allow sufficient slip for most drivers, even on a track day) or all off.

So it's a giggle. Yes, it's less hilarious than the outgoing Clio 200, but it's also less wearing. In short, the ST is just where Ford intended it to be. If you're looking for an entertaining hot supermini that you could happily drive daily without it doing your head in, the Fiesta is as competent and capable as they come.

MATT PRIOR

FORD FIESTA ST-2

Price	£17,995
0-62mph	6.9sec
Top speed	139mph
Economy	47.9mpg (combined)
CO₂	138g/km
Kerb weight	1163kg
Engine	4 cyls, 1596cc, turbocharged, petrol
Installation	Front, transverse, FWD
Power	179bhp at 5700rpm
Torque	199lb ft at 1900-4000rpm
Gearbox	6-spd manual
Fuel tank	42 litres
Boot	276/960 litres
Wheels	7.5Jx17in, alloy
Tyres	205/40 R17

MANUFACTURER'S CLAIMED FIGURES

Porsche Cayenne Turbo S

Uprated, 542bhp version of the Cayenne Turbo packs 911 Carrera S pace (for a huge price tag)

THERE WILL NO doubt be some who see the new Porsche Cayenne Turbo S as nothing more than a four-wheeled irrelevance – a plaything. And with a price tag of £107,460, an expensive one at that.

But they're missing the point of what is perhaps the most capable off-roader ever built. Consider the facts:

here's a car that weighs a considerable 2215kg and yet can dispatch the benchmark 0-62mph sprint in just 4.5sec – a time that matches that of the latest Porsche 911 Carrera S. Even with less-than-flattering aerodynamics, it also manages to achieve a top speed of 176mph.

The latest of Porsche's second-generation Cayenne models can also hold its own in off-road situations. It comes with a multi-stage air suspension that gives it 273mm of ground clearance in its highest setting and some impressive four-wheel drive hardware, including the latest in electronic torque vectoring to juggle drive between individual wheels at the rear.

In pure engineering terms, it is among the most impressive road cars ever built. But that's not to say it is perfect, or that I'd even recommend it to those with the money to buy one.

Among the Cayenne Turbo S's true highlights is a lightly reworked version of the twin-turbocharged V8 petrol engine found in the standard Cayenne Turbo – a potent proposition in its own right. The same unit also sees service in the Porsche Panamera Turbo S. Among a series of subtle power-enhancing tweaks, the 4.8-litre, 90-degree V8 receives a more free-flowing inlet manifold, increased turbocharger boost pressure and remapped electronics.

V8 is reworked from Turbo, so power figure goes up by 49bhp and torque by 37lb ft

Power climbs by 49bhp, peaking at 542bhp to make this not only the fastest but also the most powerful iteration of the Porsche off-roader to ever see series production. Torque is also up by 37lb ft at 553lb ft – developed on a band of revs between 2250 and 4500rpm. Unlike in the Panamera Turbo S, which uses a seven-speed, dual-clutch PDK gearbox, the heady reserves are channelled through an eight-speed Tiptronic automatic transmission with a conventional torque converter to all four wheels.

The upgraded engine provides

PORSCHE CAYENNE TURBO S	
Price	£107,460
0-62mph	4.5sec
Top speed	176mph
Economy	24.6mpg (combined)
CO$_2$	270g/km
Kerb weight	2215kg
Engine	V8, 4086cc, twin-turbo, petrol
Installation	Front, longitudinal, 4WD
Power	542bhp at 6000rpm
Torque	553lb ft at 2250rpm
Gearbox	8-spd automatic
Fuel tank	100 litres
Boot	670 litres
Wheels	10Jx21in
Tyres	295/35 R21

MANUFACTURER'S CLAIMED FIGURES

Straight-line stability is incredible, helped in Sport mode by a lowered ride height

the Cayenne Turbo S with relaxed qualities at town speeds and extraordinary pace when the conditions allow.

It's a remarkably refined and easy car to drive in all weathers and all seasons. Best of all, though, the performance gains come without any change in combined cycle fuel consumption, which remains at 24.6mpg.

Porsche quotes incremental improvements in the 0-62mph sprint time and top speed over the Cayenne Turbo. But they fail to convey the explosive rush of acceleration you're subjected to on a heavily pegged throttle. It dispatches big distances in an urgent manner, with impressive straight-line stability. There is a somewhat firm ride that

can sometimes turn uncomfortable and introduce some nasty tyre rumble on less than smooth road surfaces, even in Comfort mode.

Direct electro-mechanical steering, superb damping control and strong grip also provide it with impressive agility for such a big car.

With the suspension switched to Sport mode, in which the ride height is lowered to 183mm to reduce the overall centre of gravity, it carves through corners with impressive directness, control and great purchase.

That said, the Turbo S lacks the sharpness and response of the much cheaper £67,147 Cayenne GTS, which on overall balance remains the pick of the line-up, even though it lacks the Turbo S's unbelievable pace.
GREG KABLE

Porsche has introduced new cabin trims for Turbo S, such as this Black/Carrera Red

Renault Zoe

Renault has bet the farm on electric cars, but the Zoe hatchback shows the risk was worth it

Zoe zips off the mark with alacrity, but its pace subsides on the way to its 84mph limit

IN LISBON'S TRAFFIC, suddenly the Zoe made sense. It waited patiently, silently at the lights, surrounded by clattery, time-served diesels that seemed like relics. The lights switched to green and the Zoe streaked ahead of a dawdling Honda to snick into a gap in the adjacent lane. This is a brilliant urban car, its pile of torque instantly available at an ankle flex and delivered with one of three selectable, synthesised and curious hums so pedestrians can hear the Zoe coming. (The hum stops above 18mph, or you can kill it completely.)

Later, out on the open road, a dawdling MPV was swiftly dispatched. Up in the hills, the Zoe cornered with conviction, staying flat and resisting understeer. You can feel the weight, all 1468kg of it, but the centre of gravity is lower than the latest Clio's, whose platform the Zoe shares. That's because the 22kWh, 400V battery pack is spread under the floor, so the Zoe is a proper five-seater with a normal-sized boot.

That friskiness on getaway fades significantly as speed rises, and the the upper limit is set at 84mph to conserve the battery and prevent the motor from over-revving. But there's enough urge here for you not to crave more, even in Eco mode, which stifles the scorching starts but feels fine on the open road while adding another 10 per cent or so to the range.

On which vital subject, the official EU test regime credits the Zoe with a 130-mile range on a full charge. Renault itself reckons on a worst-case 60 miles in winter, 90 miles in summer. Our test drive began with 81 miles promised, but a check after 22 gentle suburban miles showed 70 miles of remaining range. After a further 14 miles of rapid driving with full acceleration, the range was down to 43 miles, but after ambling for another 14 miles there was still 42 miles of range left. Overall, the Zoe went further than its range calculator initially thought it would.

Among its range-extending devices is a reversible air-con system that heats the Zoe as well as cooling it without stealing much energy from the battery. Energy recuperation from slowing or braking is very strong, too, but the integration of 'virtual' brakes with real ones isn't entirely smooth; feathering to a gentle halt takes some skill. More jolts come when the wheels fall heavily into road surface breaks, but otherwise the ride is smooth and supple on the bespoke Michelin Energy Z-E tyres.

This is an electric car that you could actually consider buying, helped by the free fitment of a home charging unit, paid for by Renault (which picks up 25 per cent of the cost) and the government (75 per cent). It also looks great, with clean, crisp, concept car lines that are futuristic but not outlandish, some subtle blue tinting of lights and badges and a calm, sleekly styled cabin with a large R-link display screen. You can pre-heat or pre-cool the cabin while charging, too.

JOHN SIMISTER

The cabin of the all-electric hatchback is styled sleekly and has a large R-link display

RENAULT ZOE DYNAMIQUE INTENS

Price	£15,195, plus battery rental from £70pm
0-62mph	13.5sec
Top speed	84mph (limited)
Range	130 miles
CO₂	0g/km
Kerb weight	1468kg
Engine	Electric motor
Power	87bhp at 3000-11,300rpm
Torque	162lb ft at 250-2500rpm
Gearbox	Single-speed, clutchless

MANUFACTURER'S CLAIMED FIGURES

Nissan Juke Nismo

Nissan's tuning arm turns the big-selling Juke crossover into a practical high-rise hot hatch for the masses and, more specifically, ardent gamers

EVER PLAYED GRAN Turismo on a Playstation? If you have, then at some point you have probably craved a Nismo. Nismo – it's short for Nissan Motorsports – is the motorsport and high-performance road-car tuning arm of Nissan, and its souped-up Skylines have been a fixture in virtual garages since the Gran Turismo video game first appeared in 1997.

But outside of Japan (where there's an annual Nismo festival attended by 30,000 people) and away from the Playstation generation, mention the Nismo name and you'll usually be met with a shrug of the shoulders.

Not to be deterred, Nismo is heading into the mainstream with, er, the Juke. The reason? It has spotted a couple of gaps in the market: one for an affordable performance brand that appeals to the mass market more than a more specialised crowd, and another to cater for the now grown-up and car-buying Playstation generation, a group mainly made up of 20 to 30-somethings who now have the income to translate their desire for virtual Nismos into reality.

If it sounds like a risk to vastly expand a business that has only ever made race cars and high-performance, highly specialised and expensive road cars in its near 50-year history, remember that the Juke was something of a risk when it was launched in 2010, with styling that was incredibly radical for a volume product, but it has been an absolute smash hit. It has shifted more than a third of a million units and helped Nissan's Sunderland plant to produce more cars in a year than any other in British history. Fittingly, Sunderland will also be home to the Juke Nismo.

So what you get is a 1.6-litre, turbocharged petrol-powered Juke producing 197bhp, with a host of revisions to the chassis and exterior, and interior styling changes to match. The result is a different kind of hot hatch, but one that's really rather good. It's certainly the best and most involving Juke this side of the very limited-run, £400,000 Juke-R, yet it remains comfortable and usable enough to be driven every day.

Take the engine, for example. Nismo's tuners have resisted the urge to turn the Juke into a hardcore torque-steering special by upping the engine output to headline-grabbing levels, and instead have offered small but noticeable increases in power and torque to give the car a subtly more urgent character.

The engine does suffer from something of a torque vacuum before the turbocharger gets fully up to speed at around 2000-2500rpm, but keep it above this and that extra urgency is delivered in a linear fashion to the front wheels via a six-speed manual gearbox. It's an urgency that can still be felt when settled at motorway speeds, and some drivers might appreciate a taller top ratio at times. An all-wheel-drive version mated to a CVT transmission is also available.

What would add a real sense of occasion is a fruiter exhaust note – as it is, it's simply not special enough for a performance car. Aurally, things do improve when Sport mode is selected, one of three driving modes, alongside Eco and Normal, that also adjusts throttle response and steering feel. Overall, the steering is much improved over the standard Juke's, with a more direct and less artificial feel at the rim.

The Juke's ride is firm but never uncomfortable and it feels like a car that has been set up to deal with Britain's scarred road surfaces – which, thanks to input from the Cranfield technial centre, it has.

Body control is also excellent and roll is well controlled when driving within the Juke's limits. It's something of an achievement to make a car so relatively tall for its size feel quite so planted and agile.

Really press on and you'll get some

Red and black trim and use of Alcantara inject a sporting tone into the Juke's cabin

The Juke Nismo is designed to cater for the now grown-up and car-buying Playstation generation

The engine responds urgently above 2500rpm

Body roll is well contained and predictable

The Juke Nismo feels well planted in corners

understeer and slip and spin from the front wheels, but then the Juke Nismo has been tuned for the mainstream so that's entirely acceptable and to be expected. The really rewarding driving experience can be found when driving quickly and smoothly, and you don't have to push to the limit for the Juke Nismo to raise a smile.

Where the car does feel sufficiently sporty is inside the cabin. There are new sports seats that grip firmly – so firmly, in fact, that they'll give you a numb bum if you sit in them for long enough. The Alcantara-wrapped steering wheel and red-and-black-trimmed cabin are subtler mods but no less welcome in adding to the sporty feel, and they help to distract from the otherwise plasticky nature of the Juke's interior.

A good car, then, the Juke Nismo, and it stands out both as something genuinely different and as a good-value and altogether more involving alternative to a Mini Countryman Cooper S. Certainly don't cancel your order for a Renault Clio RS or Ford Fiesta ST, though, as those cars are significantly more focused and cater to a more specialised customer base.

Not that this is to dismiss the Juke Nismo. On the contrary, it means that Nissan has nailed its brief by creating model that the mass market can appreciate, rather than just appealing to the more hardcore enthusiast.

MARK TISSHAW

App appeal for the Playstation generation

A novel idea, this. Nissan has created a Nismo iPad app specifically for the Juke Nismo that takes its inspiration from both the large digital readout in the GT-R's centre console and Nismo's presence in video games. An iPad can be mounted on the Juke's centre console and connected to the car's on-board computer via Bluetooth. It then displays a whole host of readings including engine temperature, g-forces and lap times. This can then be shared with the wider Nismo community via Facebook and Twitter, so the whole world can hear how many g you pulled while lapping the M25.

NISSAN JUKE NISMO	
Price	£20,395
0-62mph	7.8sec
Top speed	134mph
Economy	40.9mpg (combined)
CO₂	159g/km
Kerb weight	1295kg
Engine	4 cyls in line, 1618cc, turbocharged, petrol
Installation	Front, transverse, front-wheel drive
Power	197bhp at 6000rpm
Torque	184lb ft at 2400-4800rpm
Gearbox	6-spd manual
Fuel tank	46 litres
Wheels	18in, alloy
Tyres	225/45 R18, Continental ContiSport Contact5

MANUFACTURER'S CLAIMED FIGURES

Caterham Seven R600

Supercharged Seven is the fastest yet, but it's only for the track – for now

FOURTH GEAR, MEDIUM revs, straight line, full power. Frantic wheelspin. This is mental. Welcome to the Caterham Seven R600.

The R600 is a racing car for those who think the R300, currently top of the racing Sevens tree, isn't fast enough. Apparently a lot of competitors think that of the highly tuned, naturally aspirated R300. But instead of using the even more highly tuned, road-only R500, the new, race-only R600 (keep up) has a supercharger strapped to its 2.0-litre Ford Duratec engine so it makes 275bhp. To say it's quick would be something of an understatement.

But that's also true of the R500, which already makes an unshabby 263bhp. So why the new model rather than just going racing with the R500? Because, says Caterham, the speed gains of the R500 are marginal given the blurry revs it needs, while consistently running near its 9000rpm upper limit brings a reliability compromise. The R600 –

with its peak power at 7500rpm – is less stressed and torquier, with 200lb ft instead of the R500's 177.

That means the R600 will pootle along at 20mph for car-to-car photography without a care in the world. Most racing cars would be spitting, complaining and grumbling at the nasty, low-revolution chore, but the R600 is a happy bunny.

Avon race rubber sits on 13-inch wheels

Caterham has not announced plans to make a road version, but its race models usually adopt number plates once they've been track proven. The supercharged Duratec engine already feels flexible enough for the job.

And the rest of the hardware? Well, that's a touch less adaptable for the road. Caterham wanted the R600 to be much quicker than the R300 – about four seconds per typical lap is the ambition – so there are Bilstein race dampers, a full roll cage, a Sadev sequential six-speed gearbox (allowing clutchless upshifts), a limited-slip differential and, in championship races, uses slick Avon tyres. During our test, at a dank Blyton Park in Lincolnshire, Caterham's demonstrator is fitted with race wets, which is just as well.

Just like a supercharged Ariel Atom, the R600 is the sort of car in which you think you've reached the end of the throttle's travel, only to find there's rather more to come. And, as in the Atom, the urge – irresistible

Track-only R600 produces 275bhp and weighs just 550kg; like all good Sevens, it's grippy yet adjustable and utterly trustworthy

Nothing in the cockpit you don't need for racing. Sequential manual Sadev gearbox will happily change up without the clutch

Forcing the issue

FOR NOW, CATERHAM thinks a turbocharged engine isn't right for a lightweight sports car due to the boosty nature of the power delivery. It believes, instead, that the linear response of a supercharger is the way forward, so it has adapted the 2.0-litre Ford Duratec motor it helped to develop for the SP/300.R track car. In order to manage the forced-induction engine's heat output, the R600 gets a new nose with a vastly increased cooling capacity.

The R600 also gets a new, lighter sequential gearbox. The Sadev unit will accept clutchless upshifts, although downshifts still want clutch use and, ideally, a throttle blip.

CATERHAM SEVEN R600

Price	£44,995
Top speed	153mph
0-60mph	2.6sec
Economy	na
CO$_2$	na
Kerb weight	550kg
Engine	4 cyls in line, 1999cc, supercharged, petrol
Installation	Front, longitudinal, RWD
Power	275bhp at 7500rpm
Torque	200lb ft at 6500rpm
Gearbox	6-spd sequential manual
Fuel tank	32 litres
Boot	na
Wheels	13-inch, alloy
Tyres	175/530 R13 (f), 200/565 R13 (r), Avon slicks

MANUFACTURER'S CLAIMED FIGURES

and relentless – arrives instantly. In these conditions, traction is not an R600 strong point, but on slicks, during a typical race season, it must be extraordinary. Twenty R600s all heading towards Paddock Hill Bend at full chat? It must be one of club racing's most entertaining moments. Even in slippery conditions it's impressive. Grip is strong and the steering is heavy, super-direct and accurate. Throttle response is

sharp and linear, while the brakes are powerful.

The R600's handling balance – because it's easier to get heat into the rear tyres than the fronts today – errs towards a touch of understeer, which can be neutralised on the way into corners with a trailed brake or, better still, with a boot of throttle. Then the R600 displays the handling tendencies of the best Sevens: utterly faithful, benign and communicative,

allowing you to stay on the gas and ride out the slide. Within two laps I was happy to exit any of Blyton's corners crossed up. There aren't many lightweight road cars, let alone race cars, in which do that so happily.

Doing it with 20 other R600s around must keep you on your toes. They asked for a faster Caterham Seven to race. And my goodness, they've been given one.

MATT PRIOR

Ariel Atom 3.5

Revisions to the chassis and engine intensify the rewards that this driving machine offers

VERSION 3.5, THEN. Sounds a bit 'software update', but Ariel doesn't like to change the big number unless it's using a new engine. And given that it has shepherded a couple of hundred of the old Honda Type R donkeys into various lock-ups around the West Country, that's a little while off.

Even so, the extra '.5' signals some fairly significant changes to the now-familiar Atom design. The most visible elements of the chassis are no different, but metal has been tweaked at the rear, around the engine mounts and rear suspension mounts, leaving the frame 15 per cent stiffer, torsionally, than an Atom 3. There are new springs and dampers, too, and the steering has been revised to make it less frenetic on centre (see sidebar). The steering is the biggest change. I'll come back to that in a moment.

Also, there's more power for the supercharged engine. Ariel is modest about outputs and now claims 310bhp at 8400rpm. But truth be told, when it was claiming 300bhp,

the blown 2.0-litre engine would put out anything up to 10 per cent more than that. More significant than the output, then, is that the by-wire throttle map has been tweaked, aimed at improving the linearity of response. Which didn't feel tardy before.

Visually, the biggest changes are longer front bodywork (or what constitutes bodywork in Ariel terms) and new headlights, repeaters on the front wings and rear lights. A new LCD dashboard unit features, too, showing which gear you're in. This is a handy reminder, because all gears tend to do the same thing

in a supercharged Atom: bring the horizon closer at a generally alarming rate of knots.

That much hasn't changed. The Atom still pootles around very benignly when you want it to, fizzes along at low revs and is ludicrously fast at higher speeds. The throttle response feels a touch improved, it's true, but to be honest the car doesn't feel any quicker to me. Still, these things are relative. It's like having seven pints instead of six: the result is pretty much the same either way.

In fact, it's the pace of a supercharged Atom that has

The new dashboard display shows which gear you're in; new headlights are effective

Revisions make the steering feel less frenetic without compromising the car's agility

An Atom has everything you need to enjoy an intensely engaging driving experiencee

The steering committee

BUMP STEER IS the tendency for a car's front wheels to steer as the suspension is compressed. It's not always a desirable trait. As toe-out increases as you wind lock on and load up the suspension, you can increase understeer, too, for example.

But Ariel has, with the Atom 3.5, dialled in more toe-out, so that in a straight line, as the suspension is compressed, the front wheels point further out and promote stability, reducing the hyperactivity of what was – and remains – a very fast steering rack. The trick is to do this while not sacrificing agility or increasing understeer; Ariel thinks the Atom feels 'calmer' without becoming more understeery. And although it's much improved already, Ariel says there's still more to come.

sometimes given the chassis some work to do. An Atom 3 is generally excellent already, with good steering and an adjustable chassis. But these improvements highlight what we didn't really think needed addressing until we tried the altered version. The steering was already extremely feelsome, responsive and hugely direct, at 1.7 turns lock to lock.

But as pace rose, so too did a little nervousness at the straight-ahead. It kept you on your toes, but I'd never thought a great deal of it until I tried the 3.5. The increased toe-out under compression makes the steering far more stable, leaving it less frenetic without compromising agility.

It's a boon on both road and track. You can now relax your grip on the wheel more without fear that the Atom will dart aside come the next bump. And, as a result of that, you can concentrate on enjoying yourself

more. No fun has been sacrificed here. The extra straight-line stability hasn't had a notable effect on handling, either. There's a touch of understeer on the way in, followed by a touch of oversteer on the way out, both totally to the degree that you want. The improved steering just allows you greater, more relaxed access to it, which, in turn, has made a lovely sports car even better.

MATT PRIOR

ARIEL ATOM 3.5 SUPERCHARGED

Price	£38,000
0-62mph	2.7sec
Top speed	155mph
Economy	25.0mpg (est)
CO₂	na
Kerb weight	550kg
Engine	4 cyls, 1998cc, supercharged, petrol
Power	310bhp at 8400rpm
Torque	236lb ft at 7200rpm
Gearbox	6-spd manual
Fuel tank	40 litres
Boot	na
Wheels	7Jx15in (f), 7Jx16in (r)
Tyres	195/50 R15 (f), 225/45 R16 (r)

Mercedes CLS63 Shooting Brake

With 550bhp and 590lb ft, this artfully crafted CLS load lugger packs serious AMG firepower

FROM A POLITE distance the CLS63 AMG Shooting Brake may seem like a jolly expensive, niche-filling folly. In fact, sitting across the Mercedes-Benz dealership in an E63 AMG estate, a car with a smaller price tag, shared underpinnings and far more space in the back where it matters, you could be excused for thinking the model's new clothes really are only fit for the most self-aggrandising emperor.

And yet... circle the Shooting Brake slowly, sympathetically, and it's hard not to fall into the gravitational pull of its design orbit. If the original CLS was meant as a style antidote to the E-class saloon's three-box conservatism, the new Shooting Brake is the perfect emollient to the E-class estate's bulky derriere. Tapering the rear may have chiselled a full 400 litres from the total load space compared with the E-class wagon, but the visual effect is considerable.

Similarly, its twin-turbo 5.5-litre V8 could be considered the perfect remedy for the car's very real 1955kg

conundrum. With 550bhp and 590lb ft of torque, it's good for 0-62mph in 4.3sec. As with the regular, 518bhp CLS63, this is a very fast car indeed. The extra power means the Shooting Brake's 85kg weight penalty is rendered meaningless, and a limiter is required to prevent this pseudo-estate from surging beyond 155mph.

Like all AMGs equipped with the firm's MCT seven-speed automatic gearbox, there's an innate reticence in manual downshifts that makes paddle-shifting this Goliath far less of a pleasure than it should be. It makes a far better fist of its duties when left to its own devices, although the

default Comfort mode is arguably too sluggardly. There is, however, something appealing about having to wind the baritone V8 into a crank frenzy from the standing start of a lazier throttle map.

Sport gives a superior mix of response and ratio selection and, assuming you couldn't give a stuff about the claimed 28mpg potential (and if you forked out the £97k for our test car then you probably won't), should be the default mode for everyday use.

Where you want to position the adjustable dampers on AMG's Ride Control is a thornier issue. As with most of its brethren, the CLS63's ride

Seats up, the boot holds 590 litres; V8 produces 550bhp; standard wheels are 19in

Sleek, tapering lines compromise load space in favour of an appealing aesthetic, while a firm ride translates into impressive agility

Detail finish in the cabin is up to Merc's exemplary standards. Our heavily optioned test car came in at a mighty £97,000

quality, even at its most doughy on standard 19-inch wheels, is hardly imperious. Arguably some of the mored aged spines destined to appear on the Shooting Brake's waiting list will expect better bump-eating pliancy for their investment, but at least the Shooting Brake is able to translate its enduring rigidity into duly engrossing agility.

True, space and isolation are required to throw almost five metres of Merc around with abandon, but find the right stretch of road and exuberant chassis poise bubbles to the surface. Throw in traction-deficient winter tyres and an optional limited-slip rear diff and the CLS63 becomes a two-tonne arcade game with springy steering to match.

Such wanton hooliganism has already made the '63' generation a spectacular vintage, and once again it leaves you with more affection for the Shooting Brake than would normally be appropriate for such a paunchy tribute to Germanic excess.

Truthfully, it's rather hard not to get a little wrapped up in the bare-faced brilliance of it all. If you can make your peace with the limited load space and attribute the gearbox's ponderousness and comfort shortfall to a personality quirk, there is a huge quantity of car here to enjoy.

NIC CACKETT

MERCEDES-BENZ CLS63 AMG SHOOTING BRAKE

Price	£83,030
0-62mph	4.3sec
Top speed	155mph
Economy	28.0mpg (combined)
CO_2	235g/km
Kerb weight	1955kg
Engine	V8, 5461cc, twin-turbo, petrol
Power	550bhp at 5250rpm
Torque	590lb ft at 2000-4500rpm
Gearbox	7-spd automatic
Fuel tank	80 litres
Boot	590-1550 litres
Wheels	9Jx19in (f), 10Jx19in (r)
Tyres	255/35 R19 (f), 285/30 R19 (r)

Peugeot 208 GTI

Performance version of Peugeot's latest supermini looks to restore the firm's tarnished legacy of GTI-badged hot hatches to 205 GTI levels

FIRST VERDICT

Very desirable performance hatch, but it lacks ultimate feedback

★★★★☆

SO GOOD

- Handling balance
- Flexible engine
- Decent ride comfort

NO GOOD

- Sonically flat
- Inherited styling
- Aloof steering

TESTER'S NOTE

Once disengaged, the traction control doesn't continually remind you it's off. Bravo, Peugeot. NC

WHEN IT COMES to the business of successfully attaching the letters 'G', 'T' and 'I' to a cogent product, Peugeot has had more false dawns than Microsoft. For every virtuous edition of Windows there seem to have been at least three Vista-like shoeboxes of awfulness. But while Renault, as we have already seen, can barely distance each new hot Clio from the shining brilliance of the previous car, Peugeot has to skip back generations to the 205 like a faltering NASA spokesman continually referencing the Apollo moon landings.

Mercifully, the manufacturer is prepared to admit that the latest 208 GTI is not intended as the second coming. Rather than catering to the 205 GTI's spirited scamp ethos, the latest model is merely a lower, leaner and quicker version of the current 208 supermini, calculated to snare a likely older audience with a more subtle approach to supermini hot hatchery.

Many of its additions, then, are customary, and can be listed without

surprise. Unlike some demonically tweaked rivals, the GTI is only gently differentiated from its lesser siblings, so whether you like its styling or not will depend on what you think of the donor car. The slightly wider track (10mm more at the front, 20mm at the rear) is just about picked out by slender arches and skirts, and a backwards baseball cap of a spoiler.

Beneath the bonnet is PSA's familiar turbocharged 1.6-litre petrol engine, now running its higher 197bhp output. Around that, Peugeot has installed a reinforced front subframe, fatter struts, sports springs, tauter dampers and beefier anti-roll bars, with bigger brakes and revised steering settings helping to better control the show.

As well as all the adding, the GTI benefits from some subtraction. At 1160kg, the car is 165kg lighter than the lardy 207 GTI – not featherlight by any stretch of the imagination, but an improvement nonetheless, especially considering that it's reasonably well

GTI shares the standard 208's basic cabin architecture, including a steering wheel at odds with the instrument panel; modest exterior styling changes add a touch of muscle to the b

PEUGEOT 208 GTI	
Price	£18,895
0-62mph	6.8sec
Top speed	143mph
Economy	47.9mpg (combined)
CO$_2$	139g/km
Kerb weight	1160kg
Engine	4 cyls, 1598cc, turbo, petrol
Installation	Front, transverse, FWD
Power	197bhp at 5800rpm
Torque	203lb ft at 1700rpm
Gearbox	6-spd manual
Fuel tank	50 litres
Boot	285 litres
Wheels/tyres	7Jx17in/205/45 R17

MANUFACTURER'S CLAIMED FIGURES

equipped with 17-inch alloys, DAB radio, dual-zone air-con and rear parking sensors as standard.

Inside, memory of the standard 208's tin-box clunkiness is swiftly expunged. Admittedly, the GTI is afflicted with the same dislocated interior – instrument cluster half-hidden by the helm, an afterthought of a multimedia screen and glossy fascia looking anything but – yet the important things ring true. The gearknob is a fistful of indented metal, the steering wheel is baby-armed in rim width but petite in diameter and the sports seats both cosset and cradle really rather brilliantly.

It's a pity, then, that the soundtrack doesn't quite share the same billing. While receiving the same engine as the RCZ coupé, the 208 doesn't get that car's trick exhaust, which means there's not much to embellish the four-pot's rather characterless drone. Out and about, though (and in line with Peugeot's game plan), it's a hospitable unit. The GTI doesn't suffer from the 208's lack of driveline refinement – even if there is some low-down hesitation in the throttle response – and, with 0-62mph dealt with in 6.8sec, there are guts enough on tap.

What you don't get are much in the way of fireworks. The dependable rocket of 203lb ft of turbocharged torque from 1700rpm is admirable and potent, yes, but largely unwilling to deviate from its flat trajectory. Granted, our test car was very tight and forced to occasionally work at altitude, but revving it out wasn't addictive, frenzied fun – and especially so given that the aural accompaniment is a restrained confusion of whistle and whine.

The same emphasis on flexibility is recognisable in the chassis, although here, hearteningly, it is handled with a little more pizzazz. While stiffer springs have been installed, the ride height has only descended by 8mm; give the steering wheel a quick jiggle and the 208 bobs merrily on its travel rather than instantly hunting for a change of direction. This leeway helps give the GTI a degree of leniency; rougher surfaces are smoothed away somewhat and it duly rides rather well.

The downside is a touch more lean when you start to tie it on. But this, too, is neatly damped. The 208 eases organically into its grip and line and the steering is a better rudder than it is guide. However, its wooden weight is not unduly inhibited by torque steer, and its size and quickness deliver sufficient nimbleness.

The chassis willingly colludes in such eagerness. There's balance and responsiveness, and through medium-fast bends the sense is that the car is pivoting at midships. Doubtless for some tastes there won't be enough susceptibility to mid-corner throttle adjustments, but there's sufficient rear-axle involvement to help trim the angle of attack. Try harder still and the 208 will cock a showboating back wheel until excess power cheerily spins up the inside front tyre.

This is, as it was meant to be, a congenial little hot hatch. It's easily bearable around town, usable on a commute and just enough of a giggle when the whim or right occasion arises. Peugeot was once a master at balancing these attributes, and there's evidence here to suggest that the hot 208 can take on the Clio RS 200 Turbo and Fiesta ST with its head held high. Welcome back to GTI, Peugeot.
NIC CACKETT

BMW 320d Gran Turismo

Can this bigger and more practical 3-series variant justify its price premium over the Touring?

FIRST VERDICT

The most spacious and practical 3-series yet. Diesel is noisy, though

★★★★⯪☆

SO GOOD

- Spacious, attractive cabin
- Versatile, well planned boot
- Tidy handling, mostly supple ride

NO GOOD

- Diesel noisier than in the saloon
- Ride can crash and heave
- Overly light steering

TESTER'S NOTE

This is a hatch with no rear wash/wipe. BMW's excuse? It's a coupé and they often do without. Hmm. **RB**

SPACE: YOU GET a lot of it in a BMW 3-series GT. Especially in the rear seat, and the boot, too. Unless you're familiar with riding on the back bench of some of BMW's biggest machines, you'll be quite unused to legroom on this scale, and if three occupy it, they'll make the surprise discovery that the arrangement will be tolerable for more than half an hour. This is the new 3-series for families that need more room than a 3-series Touring or a 5-series saloon can offer.

It's not the most handsome BMW, but if you consider it as a rakishly sporty, five-door MPV-coupé, its appeal becomes easier to understand. Especially when you learn that this car was born out of a delve into 3-series buyers' desires. That's why this car is unusual for being a taller sports hatch of a kind that, in the premium segment, has no direct equivalent. As for calling it a GT, those letters have been liberally applied for decades.

It's hugely practical. The boot is larger than a Touring's, at 520 litres, and very large indeed when the rear seats are felled to reveal 1600 litres of stowage. It's a shame that the backrests merely drop on to their cushions rather than tumbling with the seat base to form a bulkhead and a flat floor, but there's no question that you can get a lot in here. Each portion of the split backrest descends with the tug of a handle, although you must hump it back upright yourself. Versatility is further improved by a backrest that locks into 15 different positions across 19deg, potentially

allowing it to swallow that pesky chest of drawers without dropping the seats. The boot provides an under-floor well, load-securing rails, hooks and lashing eyes, and the rigid two-piece rear parcel shelf stows below the deck floor.

All GTs have electric tailgates – just as well, because it's a hefty structure – and waggling a foot under the rear bumper sends it rising skywards. Equally obscure, though, is a release button buried near the driver's door that few will spot.

The reason for all this extra space is

Lots of room for rear passengers and their luggage; backrests adjust in 15 positions

The 3-series GT handles very tidily, especially fitted with electronic M Sport dampers

This view will be familiar to anyone who has driven 3-series saloon or Touring variants

quite simple: the GT is a much bigger car (see separate story, right). You also sit at much the same height as an X1 driver. Of course, this means that this 3-series GT has a higher centre of gravity than a Touring, besides being a heftier beast. So what does that do to the dynamics?

According to GT project leader Martin Delitz, much effort has been expended maintaining the 3-series' agility, although comfort has also been a priority for this more family-oriented machine. And fitted with the £750 electronic M Sport dampers – a must-buy for any keen 3-series driver – the GT provides an almost loping pliancy, although ridges and bigger bumps occasionally provoke an unseemly thumping not present in the saloon. Some crests provoke a curious vertical bounce, too.

Firm it up from Comfort to Sport and little of that overall suppleness is lost, roll is usefully checked and the 2.0-litre diesel drivetrain roused from its occasionally near-indolent low-rev, high-geared economising strategy. The steering, which feels overly light in Comfort, muscles up to provide a sometimes slightly springy resistance, but a better than average impression of the topography beneath. And on these settings, the GT hides its higher-set mass well through corners, to exploit a 50/50 weight distribution that provides bursts of light entertainment that are limited more by the engine than any significant dynamic shortfalls.

And there's no question that BMW's 2.0 oil-burner is greying with age. It's too prominent at idle, too prominent when revved and, well, just too prominent generally. It's fairly smooth and its torque curve well spread, but in a car called GT, it's not especially quick. Performance is brisk enough for the urban battle and it's a relaxed cruiser, especially with those eight ratios, but this engine does its work without huge panache.

The transmission is more impressive, never hunting despite its multiple gears, which are selected with subtly enthusiastic verve in Sport. You can occasionally do a better job yourself across undulating twists, the paddle-shifters well placed for speedy tweaking, but this is a 'box that chooses well. And in fuel-saving Eco-pro mode, it pursues a low-rev, high-geared economy-eking strategy that might yield the odd laboured grumble from up front but promises very decent fuel consumption.

If you're a regular 3-series driver, the rest of the GT package will be familiar. As with the saloon and the Touring, you can choose from SE, Sport, Modern and M Sport trims – SE and M Sport are expected to predominate. The GT bodystyle costs £1300 more than the Touring and £2600 more than the saloon, so you need to be certain that you want the extra space and versatility. The M Sport package is well worth having because it significantly improves the GT's look, too.

So it's not a cheap 3-series, nor the most handsome, and the sometimes troubled ride and noisier engine must be factored in. But as a set of versatile family wheels of lightly sporting flavour, this 3-series is the best yet.

RICHARD BREMNER

That's about the size of it

THE GT IS a significantly bigger car than the 3-series Touring. Its wheelbase is 110mm longer, the overall length is 200mm greater, and it is 79mm taller and 17mm wider. The driver also sits 59mm closer to the sky than a regular 3-series driver. Bigger wheels (18s as standard) provide 15mm of this added height, the suspension another 20mm and the seat mountings the rest. On the structural front, localised body strengthening largely compensates for the rigidity-threatening tailgate aperture besides optimising the car's dynamic performance, and an extra rear link between the body and axle assembly improves rear wheel location.

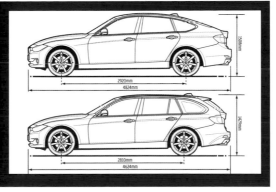

BMW 320D GRAN TURISMO SE SPORT AUTO	
Price	£32,970
0-62mph	7.9sec
Top speed	140mph
Economy	57.6mpg (combined)
CO_2	129g/km
Kerb weight	1575kg
Engine	4 cyls, 1995cc, turbodiesel
Installation	Front, longitudinal, RWD
Power	182bhp at 4000rpm
Torque	280lb ft at 1750-2750rpm
Gearbox	8-spd auto
Fuel tank	57 litres
Boot	520-1600 litres
Wheels	18-inch, alloy
Tyres	224/45 R18

MANUFACTURER'S CLAIMED FIGURES

Future cars we just can't wai

From urban runabouts to futuristic hypercars, these are the cars we'll be writing about, and lusting af

Audi R10

AUDI IS PREPARING TO enter the exclusive realm of high-end hypercar manufacturers with a spectacular 600bhp-plus, four-wheel drive R10 flagship model inspired by its latest Le Mans-winning R18 race car.

The high-tech two-seater, which is conceived to sit above the second-generation R8, aims to provide a direct link between the German car maker's high-profile motorsport activities and the vast road car side of its business.

Among the R10's planned highlights are a high-powered diesel-electric drivetrain, a dual-clutch automatic gearbox and the very latest in torque-vectoring-assisted quattro four-wheel drive.

According to Autocar's sources, R10 will centre around a newly developed carbonfibre monocoque structure and body featuring styling cues linking it directly with the aggressive-looking R18 race car.

Power is set to come from a turbocharged 3.0-litre V6 diesel engine, which will drive the rear wheels through a seven-speed dual-clutch automatic gearbox. It produces 309bhp and 479lb ft in standard form but various tweaks, including the adoption of a new induction system, lightweight internals and new crankcases, are likely to lift the unit's reserves to more than 420bhp and 515lb ft, according to one source.

Together the diesel engine and electric motor are planned to provide a combined output of more than 600bhp and 737lb ft of torque. We're very keen…

Why 2014 will be a great year for cars

Vauxhall Corsa

The fifth-gen Corsa is expected to take its design inspiration from the rakish Astra GTC. Power should come from highly efficient, turbocharged, small-capacity petrol and diesel engines as Vauxhall continues its efforts to improve its powertrains. Expect a continuation of the supermini's fine dynamics and a lighter body.

Mini

The third-generation Mini will take the brand into more family friendly territory than ever before by offering an even wider range of models and body styles. The staple three-door hatch will lead the way, and will be followed by no fewer than nine spin-offs, including a new interpretation of the Clubman estate and Mini's take on the MPV.

Ford Mondeo

It should have been with us in 2013, but Ford has pushed the all-new Mondeo back to 2014. The look doesn't stray too far from today's, but it has grown in length and height. Ford claims the Mondeo has again been conceived as a driver's car. As part of the 'One Ford' policy, the European and Asian-market Mondeo and the US Fusion have merged.

AUTOCAR
IMAGE

Volkswagen Golf R

PACKING 286BHP, THE forthcoming Volkswagen Golf R will be the most powerful regular production Golf in history.

The Golf R will crown the Mk7 Golf range, following closely behind the new VW Golf GTI. Closely related to the latest Audi S3, the Golf R's 2.0 TSI engine produces 286bhp and 280lb ft, according to well-placed insiders.

When equipped with a six-speed dual-clutch automatic gearbox, the Golf R will be able to crack 0-62mph in just 5.0sec and reach a limited top speed of 155mph. The Golf R will again be all-wheel drive and is said to weigh about 1200kg.

Despite the increased performance over the old 267bhp Golf R, its economy is said to have improved to 40.4mpg and CO_2 emissions cut to 163g/km.

Volvo XC90

IT SEEMS LIKE it has been around forever, but 12 years on, the XC90 – for many years, Volvo's best-seller – will finally be replaced in 2014.

The new version will be the first car based on Volvo's new Scaleable Product Architecture (SPA) platform, which will underpin all future Volvos from the S60 upwards. The new XC90 is marked by very short overhangs and a blunt, upright front end, said to be a nod to the Volvos of the 1970s and 1980s.

These are exciting times for revitalised Volvo, which will no longer build five, six and eight-cylinder engines and is well underway with its plans to roll-out a new series of engines.

The China-owned brand will rely on the VEA four-pot engines and hybridisation to power the SPA-based models. Volvo also says it is investigating a flywheel KERS (kinetic energy recovery system), probably working on the rear wheels, as part of the SPA component set.

AUTOCAR
IMAGE

Mercedes-Benz C-class

A vital car for Stuttgart, the new C-class must raise its game to challenge the latest 3-series, so great visual drama is promised, as are more powerful, more efficient engines and improved dynamics. The fourth-gen C-class will be offered with the latest in-car networked internet connectivity. The C63 AMG will get a new turbocharged 4.0 V8 powerplant.

Renault Twingo

Renault's revival continues apace, and this new baby car, developed with partner Mercedes-Benz alongside the new-generation Smart family, looks set to make waves. Like today's Smart platform, it uses a rear-mounted engine driving the rear wheels. Renault has a long history of building compact rear-engined cars such as the Renault 8.

Mazda MX-5

The next MX-5 and Mazda's latest SkyActiv engine and powertrain technology could make very good bedfellows. Mazda is targeting an ambitiously low weight of 800kg for the sports car, and the compact, efficient SkyActiv technology could help it achieve this aim. A power output of 130bhp from a 1.6-litre engine has been suggested.

FORMULA 1'S GREATEST INNOVATIONS

Motor racing is a high-speed test bed, but not all the ideas are successful. **Joe Saward** looks at some of the most ingenious and downright bonkers grand prix concepts

Six-wheelers

The Tyrrell team was looking for ways to reduce the frontal area of its F1 cars and chief designer Derek Gardner came up with the idea of having four small wheels at the front. The theory was that its four tiny ten-inch front wheels would increase mechanical front-end grip – with more rubber on the road – and thus eliminate understeer while at the same time improving cornering and braking. The car won in Sweden in 1976, but this turned out to be a one-off. Williams later developed a six-wheeler with four rear wheels, but it was never raced.

Rear engines

In 1950 all Formula 1 cars had front engines with chassis built from metal tubing and fuel tanks behind the driver. In 1955, however, a little-known Australian competitor called Jack Brabham appeared at Aintree, driving a Cooper with a Bristol engine mounted behind him. Cooper's rear-engined cars began winning in 1958 and Brabham won the Formula 1 World Championship in 1959 and 1960. By 1961 everyone had switched to rear-engined machinery. The switch also caused the main focus of the Formula 1 industry to shift from Italy to Britain.

Four-wheel drive

Harry Ferguson was famous for his development of tractors, but he was a man of many talents, which included being the first Irishman to build and fly his own aeroplane. In 1950 he joined forces with an adventurous young Englishman called Tony Rolt who wanted to build four-wheel drive systems for F1 cars. Ferguson saw it as a chance to promote his tractor business. The resulting F1 car was called the Ferguson P99, with which Stirling Moss took an impressive victory in the Formula 1 International Gold Cup at Oulton Park in 1961. Several other 4WD F1 cars were later built but were deemed to be too heavy.

Composite chassis

McLaren was the first team to introduce a chassis built from composite materials, which revolutionised the design of F1 cars once again. John Barnard went to the aerospace industry in Salt Lake City, Utah, where he found rocket designer Steve Nichols at Hercules Inc. They built the McLaren MP4/1. The new breed of cars were light, strong and immensely stiff – and they won.

The fan car

Gordon Murray was a man full of ideas when he became Brabham's chief designer in the early 1970s. In 1978 the Brabham team turned up in Sweden with two BT46s fitted with a large fan attached to the rear of the car. The team explained that the device was for cooling the engines, but it was soon clear that the primary aim of the fans was to suck air from beneath the cars and improve grip. The idea worked, won the Swedish GP, but was then banned.

Ground-effect

Lotus was largely responsible for the development of F1 aerodynamics from the early 1970s onwards. Working with Tony Rudd and Peter Wright, Colin Chapman went on to pioneer the use of wind tunnels in F1 and developed ground-effect, creating downforce by shaping the underside of the car to create a low-pressure area, which sucked the car to the track. The result was the elegant Lotus 79, which dominated F1 in 1978.

The monocoque

Colin Chapman was one of the great innovators in Formula 1 history. In 1962 he produced the Lotus 25, the first successful fully stressed monocoque chassis in F1. The car was three times stiffer and weighed half as much as its predecessors and Jim Clark dominated in the Lotus 25 and its elegant successor, the Lotus 33. The idea was adopted by everyone and later moved into mainstream car production.

The twin chassis

The Lotus 88 appeared shortly after the McLaren MP4/1 in 1981 and was the second all-composite F1 monocoque. This revolutionary machine was designed to circumvent the ground-effect rules by using twin chassis. The driver sat in an internal section which was softly sprung, while the external element was designed to maximize the efficiency of the ground-effect. The car was never allowed to race.

Active suspension

Team Lotus designed the first F1 active suspension, a computer-controlled system that guaranteed an unchanged, ideal flow angle. Ayrton Senna won twice in 1987 in a Lotus equipped with such a system, but it proved to be very difficult to perfect. It was not until Williams sorted out the idea that active suspension began winning races on a regular basis. Such systems were banned at the end of 1993.

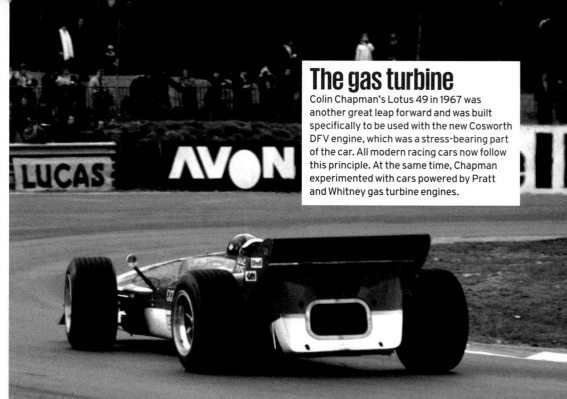

The gas turbine

Colin Chapman's Lotus 49 in 1967 was another great leap forward and was built specifically to be used with the new Cosworth DFV engine, which was a stress-bearing part of the car. All modern racing cars now follow this principle. At the same time, Chapman experimented with cars powered by Pratt and Whitney gas turbine engines.

Other wacky racers

In the 1960s F1 engineers were constantly looking for ways to squeeze more power out of their engines. BRM came up with the idea of an H16, a wildly complicated engine, which was effectively two flat-eights on top of one another. Williams developed a continuously variable transmission (CVT) in the 1990s that was banned before it could race, while Brabham tried a surface-cooled car in the mid 1970s...

IN THIS SECTION

GREAT DRIVES IN GREAT CARS

AUTOCAR'S GRAND DRIVES fall into two distinct categories, each equally valid in our quest to test, assess and compare the latest cars on the market.

The first type of test usually involves a group of cars. To appraise them properly, we need a quiet, but suitably varied, stretch of road that will enable us to test all dynamic and practical facets of the cars under scrutiny.

But then there are the drives where the experience of getting from starting point to destination is as thrilling as driving a brand new car for the first time.

Long treks such as Steve Cropley's 2000-mile odyssey from Gaydon to Marrakesh in the latest Range Rover or Andrew Frankel's cruise through California in a drop-top Bentley Continental give us an idea of a car's capabilities in extreme conditions. And as you'll see from the photo on this page, some of the scenery along the way isn't too bad either.

LIKE FATHER, LIKE SONS

Over seven generations and 50 years, the 911 has changed with the times and technology without diluting its DNA. Or has it? **Steve Cropley** drives all seven back to back

PHOTOGRAPHY PETER SPINNEY

No other car in history has so wilfully ignored engineering conventions for as long as the Porsche 911, and turned the rebellion into such glorious success. In 50 years there have been just six major alterations to that original Porsche 911 design. Each variety was introduced to meet a market change, and each has its own personality.

But the seventh and latest iteration is still amazingly closely related to the 50-year-old original – in shape, function, character and even engine note. We decided to find a prime example of each version, park all seven together to understand and appreciate the 911's visual progression, and then drive them in age order to delve into their different characters.

It's interesting to note, by the way, that during the 911's 50 years, other car makers have been encouraged to put much-loved models back into production, in newly engineered form. The Beetle, Fiat 500 and BMW Mini come instantly to mind, and the latest Volkswagen Golf continues to carry overtones of the 1974 Giugiaro-designed original. Not long ago Lamborghini produced a corrected and much modernised version of its mid-1960s Miura, as Ford did with its GT40. Renault's new Alpine-by-Caterham coupé will recall the famous Alpine A110. And Bentley has announced that it plans to 'do a 911' with the Continental GT coupé. →

← Throwing the baby out with the bath water is becoming noticeably less fashionable.

It's probably only right that the oldest 911 in our line-up should have been – historically speaking – the most distinguished of the lot. Rob Russell's fine 1966 2.0-litre coupé was one of the first four right-hand-drive 911s to reach the UK, and within weeks it had become Motor's road test car (notching a top speed of 130mph and a 0-60mph sprint time of 8.3sec). Then, for a short time, it was Porsche's London demonstrator, until it was snaffled one weekend by rally hero Vic Elford for a televised rallycross event, during which it did some highly visible fender-banging with Roger Clark in a Lotus Cortina.

Elford won the race, but the car's owners were distraught – until they noticed that the phone was ringing off the hook because customers who had seen the new Porsche on TV wanted to place orders. The car did more competition, both in rallies and even BTCC races, before being bought in the 1980s by Russell's late father. Nowadays, restored, taxed and tested, it lives in semi-retirement in Essex, although Russell was happy to bring it to a snowy Porsche Driving Centre at Silverstone, HQ for this 911 adventure.

Read Motor's road test number

43 from 1966 and you'll find much that still applies to the early 911: "Absolute solidity... designed for hard drivers... superb gearchange... cruising speeds around 90mph... enough noise to remind you that this is a sporting machine."

When you drive it in 2013, the striking thing is how usable it is. There's a bit of fluffiness at the bottom of the engine range (under 2500rpm) that surprises those used only to electronic fuel injection (this car has a pair of made-for-Porsche triple-choke Webers), but it's extremely torquey for a 2.0-litre and feels increasingly strong as you rev towards the limit of 6800rpm. The dog-leg gearchange doesn't have a modern 'defined' feel – in fact, it's distinctly rubbery – but there's a delicious mechanical action as you move it about that still makes it delightful. You just need familiarity with the gate to avoid mistakes.

The unassisted steering is terrific – surprisingly light at low speeds both because there's no engine weight to speak of over the front wheels (weight distribution is a deeply unfashionable 40 per cent front) and because the steering wheel is quite large in diameter. Once you get going, it feels perfectly weighted, with a fine feeling of connection to the road and practically no lost motion at the

The original 911 has wonderful steering / Its 2.0-litre engine is extremely torquey

This particular example has a fine motorsport history

straight-ahead. What gets politely glossed over with early Porsches is their tendency to break away abruptly at the rear, when the mass of the engine takes charge. The truth is that the front wheels are so lightly loaded that the car's initial characteristic is understeer. Only when it is pitched at speed into a corner or given everything in a very slow one will it oversteer; if it happens, it can quickly become

impossible to recover. Those who understand early 911s find them delightful. Keep the power on and the rear probably stays in line; throttle off and the tail comes rapidly around. Probably too rapidly. When cornering, the whole car seems to balance on an axis running between the inside front and outside rear contact patches. With practice, you can use this to drive with great precision, but this is

Only when pitched at speed into a corner or given everything in a very slow corner will it oversteer

1963-1973

1973-1989

Second 911 is longer but the same width

As with the original, no power steering

Power came from a 3.0 and, later, a 3.2

always a car that needs concentration, and no argument.

True to its principle of continuous development but no change for change's sake, Porsche improved the 911's engine capacity, power and 'fail safety' over about 10 years of the 'Classic's' life, putting two inches into the wheelbase in 1967, but no major body mods were made until the debut in 1975 of the outrageous, low-volume Turbo, which fed many of its differences (but not the extra-wide wheel arches) into staple 911s a year later, to make a model variously dubbed Carrera 3.0, then SC, then Carrera 3.2. The car was now 130mm (five inches) longer, but no wider and only a shade heavier, so the 200bhp available from its developed 3.0-litre engine, refined by continuous racing, made this a genuine 150mph car.

The second Porsche in our selection was arguably the most desirable from this era, a 3.2-litre Carrera, now packing 231bhp but still with a five-speed gearbox and no power steering. And still with a handbrake lever from a Beetle. I owned one of these for several years, so driving Porsche GB's freshly restored version was pure magic. This was the 911 with which Porsche sought to demonstrate its determination to keep the icon in production – after that bout of management indecision –

while it planned modernisation in the next phase. Drive the 3.2 now and you instantly feel the antiquity as keenly as the solidity; there's 2013-standard precision and tautness in the way the doors close, in the enduring durability (although not materials quality) of the cockpit fittings and in the way its firm suspension thuds tautly over bumps, rather than crashing into them like other fast cars of the time.

The Carrera 3.2 is not as delicate to steer as an original 911, and it's quite heavy at parking speeds. You have to lean forward out of the seat to slot third gear (fifth is better; it's closer) but the actual gearchange is smooth, mechanical and beautiful. The pedals are hinged on the floor (Beetle influence, still), which means that there's never enough room for your feet, but the clutch is firm and precise, while the relatively heavy brake pedal is great now and must have been utterly superb in its time.

This is a rewarding car to drive today, with an entertaining amount of poke and a terrific air-cooled engine note reaching you through the rear bulkhead and windows (open as often as possible, despite the conditions), but it's still obviously tail-heavy. The knife-edge handling is still there, but tamed somewhat by a wider rear track, bigger tyres and the application of lots of engineering brain power. →

1988-1993

Third-gen 964 brought four-wheel drive...

...plus power steering and a six-speed 'box

2000-MILE DRIVE

Range Rover SDV8

New Range Rover reveals its true colours on an epic journey from Gaydon to Marrakesh

PHOTOGRAPHY STAN PAPIOR

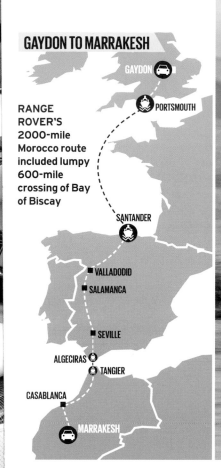

GAYDON

PORTSMOUTH

RANGE ROVER'S 2000-mile Morocco route included lumpy 600-mile crossing of Bay of Biscay

SANTANDER

VALLADODID

SALAMANCA

SEVILLE

ALGECIRAS

TANGIER

CASABLANCA

MARRAKESH

'The twin-turbo V8 diesel is almost never extended'

WHAT, WOULD YOU say, should be the top priority when you've just arrived in Morocco, having safely delivered the latest Range Rover from its Midlands home to the North African site of its international driving debut, 2000 miles south? A decent rest, perhaps, with a glass of something restorative?

Both were quickly offered when, in the gathering dusk one Friday night, I swung our 4.4-litre Autobiography SDV8 through the tall gates of Marrakesh's swish Palais Namaskar at the end of a road trip from the UK totalling 1288 miles, with another 600 sea miles thrown in for a lumpy crossing of the Bay of Biscay. However, my mind was on neither relaxation nor comestibles but – strangely, some will think – on locating one of three original Range Rovers that, I had been told, were ready to be driven at our destination.

It mattered because as someone who has attended launches for all four Range Rover generations over the past 40 years and found himself writing similar comments about each

(unique elevated driving position, unparalleled feeling of well-being, soft but controlled ride, smooth V8 torque, accurate but slightly ponderous steering), I was desperate to discover, by stepping straight from the latest Range Rover into a decent original, how true this latest model was to its celebrated beginnings. It's not often you get such a chance.

Sadly, the daylight wasn't with us. Respecting the propensity for Marrakesh's pedestrians to treat roads as footpaths, and for its motorists to drive dilapidated and ill-lit cars with an abandon that would scare even the wilder drivers of Naples or Mumbai, we decided to park the idea (and my impatience) until the next day.

The lure of driving the latest Range Rover (specifically the SDV8 in Autobiography trim) from the UK had been irresistible. Our loose plan was to pick it up on Tuesday, then drive the 120 miles from Jaguar Land Rover's Gaydon base to Portsmouth by 5pm to

Even 500 miles of driving Spanish rain couldn't dull ambience of Range Rover cockpit

catch the 24-hour ferry to Santander on the northern Spanish coast. On Wednesday night we'd drive a couple of hours into Spain, then complete the trip to Algeciras, where you cross to Africa, by the end of Thursday. On Friday we'd drive the remaining 360 miles to Marrakesh via Casablanca.

A two-hour trip from Gaydon to Portsmouth is just the sort of stroll you need to ease into a longer relationship with a new Range Rover. It allows you to set aside the excitement of the car's newness and concentrate on reality.

What lingers about the this latest generation of Range Rover is how directly it relates to the previous model. The major styling elements and proportions, the driving position and your relationship with fascia, door sills and windscreen are fundamentally the same. Sure, there are detailed enhancements all over the place, but they add up not so much to a feeling that the new car is unfamiliar, but that the outgoing (L322) model is just a bit old. Which it is, having been launched more than a decade ago.

The twin-turbo V8 diesel, at the →

Enhanced 4.4-litre diesel V8 engine provides ultra-refined, long-legged cruising

Cars aren't allowed into Marrakesh's ancient medina, but bikes (and tourists) are

← it; it still felt agile in corners but was noticeably better-riding than bigger-wheeled versions. As we closed in on Algeciras, the rain stopped for an hour or two, but it hardly mattered. Soon we were ensconced in a dockside hotel, a former convent fetchingly named the Santi Ponce. The odometer read 854.9 miles and economy had eased back to 29.7 mpg – still brilliant in my book.

On the Algeciras dockside, you get a taste of African bureaucracy. If it's your first, like me, you'll react badly to the confusion, disorganisation and competitive crowding. Veterans (I am told) stroll through it. But we queued first at one book-in booth, were diverted to another amid chaos, then were directed back to the original. By sleight of hand, we managed to jump forward a couple of dozen places, feeling not guilt but triumph. Only by such means does a person understand his private flaws and foibles.

On board the M/V Santa Cruz de Tenerife, a sign suggested we get our passports stamped by the Moroccan immigration official aboard for the purpose. On a 90-minute crossing in a half-full ferry, it should have been easy. But the bloke drank coffee and played cards for three-quarters of the crossing, until punters banging on his closed shutter became too loud to resist. There followed a mad scramble to get stamped before it was time to disembark, during which I learned that Moroccan people, although unfailingly gentle, friendly and polite, are experts at competitive queuing. We made it back to the Range Rover and drove off the ship. Although near the bow, we again found that many dozens of residents' overladen vehicles had beaten us to Tangier's swish new customs post. It took an hour to clear.

Morocco, at least initially, was disappointing. The road around

RR's lines are all-new but carry forward an unmistakable 42-year tradition

Scrawled note (right) attempts to sum up latest model

Enterprising local fixed old RR's throttle issue

Profile view shows long wheelbase of 2013 Range Rover

Tangier and down the coast to Casablanca, a new toll autoroute restricted to 75mph, was as flat and deserted as any you might encounter in large tracts of Spain, Australia or the US. Snapper Stan Papior was getting distinctly agitated – and his mood wasn't helped 280 miles later when we spent a fruitless hour looking for photographic locations in Casablanca. Only my own confidence that Marrakesh – 160 miles further on – was the gateway to the magnificent Atlas Mountains, which Winston Churchill loved to paint from his hotel room, placated our fretful on-board artiste, and made it possible to end our journey in reasonable harmony at the Palais Namaskar, just too late to try one of the original Range Rovers.

From there, things came good – very good. Marrakesh, for all its teeming car and truck traffic, punctuated by hordes of suicidal motorcyclists and pedestrians, turned out to be the most remarkable North African jewel of a city, whose ancient centre was a fascinating mêlée of sights, smells, sounds, customs and traditional businesses that seemed as they must have been 500 years ago. For Stan, prime photo locations were now fighting for priority in his head.

The next day I tried a 1971 Range Rover and did some off-roading in the 2013 one. The old car was practically the twin of the early-build, no-power-steer, four-speed, two-door model, rust-wracked model I owned 25 years ago. Twenty miles into our mountain route, while overtaking a donkey cart, I managed to break the throttle cable, but it was promptly soldered back to life by a young roadside mechanic, one of those self-trained geniuses who keep machines running decades after their Western cousins would have given up for want of spares.

It was an uplifting experience, as was my continuing drive in the old Range Rover, which, I was overjoyed to discover, did indeed still possess those unmistakable qualities ascribed to it all that time ago: a beautiful and timeless shape, a wonderful driving position, a soft and well damped ride, the beguiling elasticity of a V8 engine and – still – quite decent capability on and off the road.

Only the very finest designers and engineers can preserve a great car's key characteristics across many years. The creators of the VW Golf have consistently achieved it, and in its latest iteration the Porsche 911 is back to its best. But the 2013 Range Rover eclipses them all. Everything about it is new, yet not a single crease or widget diminishes the intangibles that make a Range Rover great. What is more, the scale of this new model's improvement over the outgoing one is certain to surprise those who drives it. Leaving Morocco, I attempted to sum up the new model in my notebook. "It's like a Range Rover," I wrote, "only much, much better."

STEVE CROPLEY

RANGE ROVER AUTOBIOGRAPHY SDV8	
Price	£94,695
0-62mph	6.9sec
Top speed	135mph
Economy	32.5mpg (combined)
CO2	229g/km
Kerb weight	2360kg
Engine	V8,4367cc, twin-turbo, diesel
Installation	Front, longitudinal, 4WD
Power	334bhp at 3500rpm
Torque	516lb ft at 1750-3000rpm
Gearbox	8-spd automatic
Fuel tank	105 litres
Wheels	8.5x20in
Tyres	255/50 R20

MANUFACTURER'S CLAIMED FIGURES

RENAULT
THE

Renault's latest Clio 200 is unlike any before it, and not just because it dispenses with a manual 'box. **Steve Sutcliffe** pits it against the Toyota GT86

PHOTOGRAPHY STUART PRICE

RIPS UP MANUAL

So back in the real world of high-performance motoring, away from the mega-buck, mega-horsepower arena of LaFerrari and McLaren's P1, the Renault Clio RS 200 Turbo is arguably 2013's most eagerly awaited car. And there are all sorts of reasons why it is so relevant to the here and now.

One: it is very much of the moment when it comes to delivering a big bang for not that many bucks. It has 197bhp and can hit 62mph in 6.7sec yet costs just £18,995 in basic form, or £19,995 in Lux trim, as tested here.

Two: at the same time, it also makes a genuine attempt not to dent the environment too much in

the process – hence the reason why it's powered by a smaller, 1.6-litre turbocharged engine that delivers 44.8mpg and just 144g/km, compared with the previous hot Clio's dirtier, thirstier, atmospheric 2.0-litre powerplant.

Three – and this is where the Clio 200 gets exceedingly contemporary indeed – it comes with a dual-clutch automatic transmission, and a dual-clutch automatic transmission only. So anyone who's in the 'I won't drive cars without a manual gearbox because paddle-shift gearboxes are for sissies' camp won't be driving a new Clio 200. Which is a fairly bold but also potentially damaging move by Renault. Only time will tell whether the →

BRAKING THE MOULD

New CLS Shooting Brake or XF Sportbrake? And is either really any better than a regular estate from Audi or BMW? **Andrew Frankel** finds the answers in Wales

PHOTOGRAPHY STUART PRICE

Shooting Brake is one of those terms that won't sit still. Its origins lie in a form of wagon tied to young horses in order to 'break' them but was then adopted by the infant motor industry to describe the kind of conveyance that might take parties game hunting on their land. It was then cast out to market niches because it was less of a mouthful just to use the word for that land and call them 'estates' instead. And there the term sat, describing a curious and scarce breed of three-door estates such as the Volvo 1800ES and Reliant Scimitar. Not that Ferrari would, but it would be historically accurate to call the FF a Shooting Brake.

But you'll find no three-door cars here, even though half use the word 'Brake' in their titles. The term has been purloined once more and now applied to what looks like yet another new car class for those seeking to maximise grace as well as space. So the real contest here is between the new Mercedes-Benz CLS350 CDI Shooting Brake and Jaguar XF 3.0 V6D S Sportbrake. But maybe the bigger question is whether putting form ahead of function is even a valid approach for such cars. So we brought a couple of our favourite conventional wagons along, the BMW 535d Touring and Audi A6 Allroad 3.0 BiTDI quattro, to keep them honest.

On paper, at least, the Brakes start with a handicap. All four cars here come with the most powerful 3.0-litre diesel engines on offer, but whereas the estates both offer better than 300bhp, the Brakes not only have a lot less power – 261bhp for the Benz, 275bhp for the Jag – but they're down on torque, too. The differences feel even more →

Among the conventional cars, the BMW and the Audi are far closer than we'd thought

← accurate to flick into a corner. In a way, the BMW's winter tyres made it even more fun than it might otherwise have been. It was more mobile at the back even than the Jaguar but without any feeling of edginess, happy to be driven on the throttle. But these are estate cars, sporting or not, and drifting ability is not high on the priority list. What we missed was that usual mid-corner incisiveness and steering precision that we'd expect from a BMW. Steering feel was not a patch on that provided by the CLS.

The Audi, frankly, was an enigma. Because of its huge torque and all-wheel drive, it turned out to be the quickest of the lot point to point. But it was also the least fun, alone in feeling nose heavy and offering so little steering interaction that it made the others feel like Lotuses.

Some may think that's a fair price to pay for the best ride of the bunch. Alone in offering air springs at all four corners (the others provide air only at the back for self-levelling purposes), it sponges away imperfections in a way more reminiscent of a Mercedes saloon than anything with rings through its nose. We'd judge the CLS as best of the rest; it's probably the firmest of the four but is sufficiently well damped to get away with it, with the BMW and Jaguar just a little more unsettled across a range of surfaces. None, it should be said, has a ride that is problematic in a substantial way.

So that's the hard-nosed bare bones of it. But can the Brakes provide something else, less easy to define but just as important to the outcome of this test: a sense of occasion or pride of ownership that the conventional estates lack?

One look at the sculpted, swooping lines of the CLS would suggest it can. The XF has lost more of its looks in its transformation from saloon to estate, but it remains a very attractive machine. But the Audi is even better looking in five-door form than four and, for sheer presence, rivals the best of the Brakes. The comparatively bland BMW is a clear fourth-place finisher in the beauty contest.

But inside it's the Jag that fails to convince. Its cabin is attractive and full of delightful features such as the rotating vents and extendable gear selector, but the driving environment is not a patch on the others. Its dials are hardest to read, its nav system simply poor by the standards of the day and its ergonomics flawed. The BMW gets all these important issues just right, offering easily the best information and navigation displays, but packages it in surroundings that look industrial and dull. For this money, a greater sense of luxury and specialness should be expected.

That sense is best provided by the Mercedes, although the Audi is not far behind. If the Allroad interior has a problem, it is simply that we've seen

As a five-seater, the CLS's boot is biggest

In two-seat guise, BMW holds 1670 litres

Audi's is the largest overall, at 1680 litres

Jaguar's swells from 550 to 1675 litres

The Mercedes provides good steering and fine balance

Tail-out fun is available in the BMW on its winter tyres

The Audi is quick and surefooted over country lanes

This Jag isn't as rewarding as other XFs in the line-up

it, or something very like it, too many times before. It all looks beautiful and works wonderfully but is now overly familiar. The CLS driving environment is a little less intuitive but even more out of the ordinary. Its quality and style brighten up every journey and, crucially, deliver fully on the promise made by its exterior.

So in the battle of the Brakes, there is a clear winner. The CLS is everything you might hope from such a car in terms of luxury and style, while offering far more than you might imagine in bald practicality. Among the conventional cars, the Audi and BMW are far closer than we'd thought, but this is Autocar and the BMW is sufficiently better to drive to overcome its weaknesses.

And what of the bigger issue? Can a Shooting Brake really act as an effective alternative estate? With a car combining cool and competence into a mix as convincing on almost all fronts as that presented by the Mercedes-Benz CLS, the answer is a clear and emphatic yes. Ⓐ

	1 Mercedes-Benz CLS350 CDI AMG Sport Shooting Brake	**2** BMW 535d M Sport Touring	**3** Audi A6 Allroad 3.0 BiTDi quattro	**4** Jaguar XF 3.0 V6 Diesel S Sportbrake
VERDICT	Impressive in almost every way that really matters	Its driving ability puts it ahead of the Audi, but only just	Beautiful and fast; with better handling it could have won	Charming, but flaws are exposed by its rivals at this price
RATING	★★★★½	★★★★☆	★★★★☆	★★★½☆
Price	£55,995	£50,155	£49,760	£51,505
0-62mph	6.6sec	5.5sec	5.6sec	6.6sec
Top speed	155mph	155mph	155mph	155mph
Economy	47.1mpg (combined)	47.9mpg (combined)	42.2mpg (combined)	45.5mpg (combined)
CO_2 emissions	162g/km	155g/km	176g/km	163g/km
Kerb weight	1910kg	1900kg	1910kg	1880kg
Engine layout	V6, 2987cc, turbodiesel	6 cyls in line, 2993cc, turbodiesel	V6, 2967cc, turbodiesel	V6, 2993cc, turbodiesel
Installation	Front, longitudinal, RWD	Front, longitudinal, RWD	Front, longitudinal, 4WD	Front, longitudinal, RWD
Power	261bhp at 3800rpm	313bhp at 4400rpm	309bhp at 3900rpm	275bhp at 4000rpm
Torque	457lb ft at 1600rpm	464lb ft at 1500rpm	479lb ft at 1450rpm	442lb ft at 2000rpm
Power to weight	137bhp per tonne	165bhp per tonne	162bhp per tonne	146bhp per tonne
Specific output	87bhp per litre	105bhp per litre	104bhp per litre	92bhp per litre
Compression ratio	15.5:1	16.5:1	16.8:1	16.0:1
Gearbox	7-spd automatic	8-spd automatic	8-spd automatic	8-spd automatic
Length	4956mm	4907mm	4928mm	4966mm
Width	1881mm	1860mm	1874mm	1877mm
Height	1416mm	1462mm	1461mm	1480mm
Wheelbase	2874mm	2968mm	2912mm	2909mm
Boot	590-1550 litres	580-1670 litres	565-1680 litres	550-1675 litres
Fuel tank	80 litres	70 litres	65 litres	70 litres
Range	660 miles	590 miles	483 miles	560 miles
Front suspension	Double wishbones, coil springs, anti-roll bar	Double wishbones, coil springs, anti-roll bar	Double wishbones, air springs, anti-roll bar	Double wishbones, coil springs, anti-roll bar
Rear suspension	Multi-link, air springs, anti-roll bar	Multi-link, coil springs, anti-roll bar	Multi-link, air springs, anti-roll bar	Multi-link, air springs, anti-roll bar
Brakes	Ventilated discs (f), ventilated discs (r)	Ventilated discs (f), ventilated discs (r)	Ventilated discs (f), ventilated discs (r)	Ventilated discs (f), ventilated discs (r)
Wheels	9Jx19in (f), 11Jx19in (r)	9Jx20in	9.5Jx20in	9.5Jx20in
Tyres	255/35 YR19 (f), 285/30 YR19 (r)	245/45 VR18	255/40 YR20	255/35 YR20

THE PERFECT

We know the latest Porsche Cayman is good, but can it be both as engaging as a Lotus Exige and as usable as a BMW M3? **Matt Prior** is the judge

PHOTOGRAPHY STUART PRICE

SPORTS CAR?

Pity the rivals to the Porsche Cayman, those few that it has. The latest version of the Cayman, which went on sale earlier this year, remains as intelligently positioned as it was when introduced eight years ago and it's a brave company that takes it on.

When we first considered a group test involving the Cayman several months ago, we thought of two alternatives which, when we secured their loans, might stand a chance.

But as we gather on some very quiet and pleasingly sunny roads near Faro, Portugal, I opt to change the rules of this test a little. I'd like the Cayman not just to better

the BMW M3 or Lotus Exige S on breadth of all-round appeal, because I'm pretty confident that it will manage that quite easily.

Instead, I'd like it to better each of them at their specialist subject, whatever that might be.

In the Lotus's case, it's obvious enough. The look of fatigue on its driver's face as he arrives in Faro says as much. Covering 1500 miles in a Lotus whose seats don't recline, whose windows don't quite seal properly and whose wiper doesn't make complete contact with the windscreen it's briefed to clear would be bad enough even if you didn't have to stop every 180 miles for petrol. Still, I'll judge the Exige

only on what it does when it gets up into the nearby hills, where I'm confident that it'll do what we expect Lotuses to do best.

Arriving with it is BMW's M3, a performance car whose beard is so grey that BMW has taken to 'special edition' mode to keep it ticking over. (This month it's 54 'Champion Edition' cars to celebrate a successful DTM return.) It joins the other two, though, because it's on the money and, frankly, is still hugely entertaining to the extent that there is very little else with its breadth of appeal.

BMW GB doesn't keep an M3 any more, so our test car has arrived from Munich, which unfortunately

but inevitably means that it is shod with the winter tyres that are an insurance necessity in Bavaria at this time of year. So if you think that it looks undernourished in the wheel department, that's because it's running 18-inch rims and chunky rubber, rather than simply because the Merccdes-Benz C63 AMG Black Series has redefined how brawny a sports coupé can look. I'll try not to let it matter. I've spent sufficient time in M3s to know that they can be extraordinarily rewarding pieces of kit and, judging by the relatively bushy tail and bright eyes of the man who drove it from Germany to Portugal, our test example remains a pretty easy-going companion on →

When it comes to comfort, the Cayman runs the M3 close

M3's cabin is laid out for easy use and has a restrained look

With the Lotus you are buying dynamics and not ergonomics

The Exige S has superb steering and wonderful balance

The Cayman S is rewarding and hugely capable

M3 still steers and handles with class, despite its age

← a motorway, too. So is the Porsche, as it turns out. Our test car is a 3.4-litre S, with optional £1922 PDK transmission, and on the run up to the hills it proves nothing but an easy-going companion. My inclination would still be towards a manual gearbox, but the majority of S buyers opt for a two-pedal arrangement and it's now so good that you can understand why.

There are other options fitted to our test Cayman, too. Quite a few, perhaps inevitably. Some you can ignore, but some will change the dynamic demeanour of the car to the extent that they're worth listing in full. On top of the Cayman S's base £48,783, there are £1477's worth of 20-inch alloy wheels, and torque vectoring with a limited-slip differential (which I reckon you'd want, even though it's £890 and you have to add active dampers, at £971, with it). Sport Chrono Plus is another £1084 but brings with it dynamic engine mounts that lock the motor down when you're pressing on.

There are also £2226 sports seats, which are excellent, but after trying the standard items I can't say I'd bother when you're looking at a price that's already easy to put into the high 50s. Mind you, they complement a decent interior, which has the latest-gen Porsche look and feel and mostly sound ergonomics. As a place to drive from London to Faro, you'd have to say it would be preferable to the Lotus.

I know that's about as surprising as finding that it gets dark at night, and I'm inclined to cut the Exige S a bit of slack here. Its basic price doesn't do it any favours, at £52,900 before you start adding option packs, so you have to really try to remember its purpose. Then it's possible, just about, to overlook some of the finish, and the fact that the

sills are too thick and high for easy entry, and the seats too close to each other for it to be anything other than claustrophobic two up, and that the interior finish is hollow and brittle. It's a real sports car, right?

Right. To that end, it's also worth remembering that the Exige weighs just 1176kg (heavy for a small Lotus, but not heavy in normal terms) and makes 345bhp from its supercharged V6. The Porsche – despite being a touch lighter than its predecessor – is a 320bhp, 1350kg car. Remember those things, because otherwise the inevitable conclusion you'll draw is that the Cayman is simply destroying everything else in this sector.

And the BMW? Its interior still pleases, even a long time after its introduction. It's the only one here that seats four, which gives it some kind of advantage, and the rear seats even split and fold. That, coupled

with the fact that it has a brawny V8 putting out 414bhp at 8300rpm, makes it remarkably easy to justify its 1675kg kerb weight and £57,590 price when equipped, as here, with a dual-clutch automatic transmission.

And, in fact, this is the easiest bit of the test to wrap up: can the Porsche match the M3 for habitability? Well, no, not if you have more than one passenger to transport, or you like playing golf, but when it comes to ride control and general comfort, the Porsche runs the M3 close. There's a touch more road noise in the Porsche, perhaps a touch more wind noise as well, with the optional sports exhaust of our test Cayman (did I mention that? It's another £1473), which, on anything other than the lightest of throttles, emits a boom that could – could – be wearing on a long journey.

Those things are enough to leave the balance in the M3's favour, but →

The Cayman adopts the latest Porsche look and feels solid

The Exige S comes alive on demanding mountain roads

The M3 offers pace, dynamic ability and everyday usability

← I'm splitting hairs. You'd arrive no more fatigued in the Cayman after a long journey, I'm confident.

I'm getting ahead of myself. Up on these good roads, I'll turn to the M3 first, because I don't expect it to be the most rewarding drive we have here. And, especially on these tyres, that's how it turns out. Threading an M3 across twisty roads on winter tyres is like running around in sports shoes, but with a rug on top of the floor. The basics are there but undermined by a lack of precision and confidence.

It's a pity, because I can just imagine how lovely an M3 would be on roads like this, with well sighted second and third-gear corners and lots of short straights with opportunities for heavy braking and quick bursts of throttle. And even through the mush of the tyre blocks (235/40 R18s all round) there's still stuff to enjoy today: the engine's willingness to rev and rev, the inherent trustworthiness and balance of a long, front-engined, rear-wheel-drive machine.

But even if you put the BMW on hand-cut slicks, it wouldn't match the Exige S. What a machine this Lotus is. It's a piece of pure, impassioned engineering and places unrivalled feel into your hands and under your feet. Steering that's incredibly heavy at parking speeds loses its heft and takes on an intuitiveness that no other car here – arguably no other road car on sale today – can match.

And by gum it's quick; it's the fastest car here in straight acceleration and braking, no question. Lotus

claims a sub-4.0sec time to 60mph, compared with 4.6sec for the M3 and 4.7sec for the (Sport Chrono-equipped) Porsche. But it's the constant urgency that makes the gap feel bigger. It's a shame the gearshift on the manual six-speeder isn't better. The best you can say for it is that it's mostly unobtrusive and just about lets your hand keep up with the demands that the performance and chassis place on you to change gear.

In this company, the Exige's front tyre width looks quite modest (205 plays 235 on the other two), but the relatively low weight means that the Lotus seems to carry much more speed on corner entry. The Elise-based chassis of Exiges has always given them a rearward weight bias and this, plus that 345bhp, means that the Lotus wears 265-section rubber on the back (the same width as the Porsche).

It's the light front that warns of letting go first, though. Trail the brakes and keep the nose nailed into a corner and the Lotus instead goes happily neutral, but there's no limited-slip differential, so it's not inclined to throw its tail around for fun. Its handling is, if you like, too grown-up for that kind of malarkey. It's too interested in being precise and incisive to indulge in any of your stupid skids. I love it.

And so to the Porsche, a car with a limited-slip differential and a handling balance that is inclined to slip around if you want it to. In a way, it contains the finest elements of the other two cars here. Its engine is in

Lotus gripped decently; BMW used winter rubber; Cayman had optional 20-inchers

The Cayman S is deeply satisfying yet undemanding

the middle, for a start, right where it ought to be, so it displays a lovely balance – keen to neither understeer nor oversteer without provocation. Its body control is exemplary, its steering easy-going and free from unwanted kickback, as in the M3.

Maybe the steering is a bit too filtered, in fact. Perhaps it's an inevitability of moving to electric power assistance, or perhaps it's that, next to an Exige S, anything seems to lack feel. Certainly, the more miles you do in a Cayman, the less of an issue it seems. Truth is, going back to back with the unassisted rack of a Lotus will do nothing any favours.

In short, the Cayman is hugely impressive everywhere. Through its demeanour and its trustworthiness, it becomes a hugely intuitive tool. It feels slower than that headline standing-start figure would suggest, but that's not an issue; speed doesn't equal fun. The Cayman S is quick enough, all the time, with an engine that spins theatrically, responding with the sort of magic that a naturally aspirated unit knows. The twin-clutch transmission pushes upshifts through brilliantly and blips perfectly on downshifts.

Those linear responses, plus a control of its body movements that allows it to settle off of crests and into dips at the first time of asking, without a hint of harshness, mean that it's a particularly undemanding yet utterly rewarding car to drive quickly. It is the sports car refined and honed, polished to a fine sheen, but it still remains emotive thanks to the exhaust note, engine response and encouraging chassis. Fitted with that differential, it's even quite happy to indulge in being slid around, predictably and controllably.

Ultimately, does it engage quite as totally as the Lotus? By a whisker, not on these roads. And by the same margin, that whisker, an M3 remains more habitable. So there are no real losers here; each plays and stars through its strengths. But the fact is that you now need two cars, not one, to beat a Porsche Cayman.

It is everything. ▲

The Cayman is an utterly rewarding car to drive quickly

S·GO 1323

	1 Porsche Cayman S	2 Lotus Exige S	3 BMW M3
VERDICT	Possibly the most complete sports car ever made	Like nothing else on the right road. Tiring on the wrong one	Entertaining, but the sensible choice in this company
RATING	★★★★★	★★★★½	★★★★☆
Price	£50,705 (PDK)	£52,900	£57,590
0-62mph	4.7sec	3.8sec (to 60mph)	4.6sec
Top speed	175mph	170mph	155mph (limited)
Economy	35.3mpg (combined)	28.0mpg (combined)	23.7mpg (combined)
CO_2 emissions	188g/km	236g/km	205g/km
Kerb weight	1350kg	1176kg	1675kg
Engine layout	6 cyls horizontally opposed, 3436cc, petrol	V6, 3456cc, supercharged, petrol	V8, 3999cc, petrol
Installation	Mid, longitudinal, RWD	Mid, longitudinal, RWD	Front, longitudinal, RWD
Power	321bhp at 7400rpm	345bhp at 7000rpm	414bhp at 8300rpm
Torque	273lb ft at 4500-5800rpm	295lb ft at 4500rpm	295lb ft at 3900rpm
Power to weight	237bhp per tonne	293bhp per tonne	247bhp per tonne
Specific output	93bhp per litre	100bhp per litre	104bhp per litre
Compression ratio	12.5:1	10.0:1	12.0:1
Gearbox	7-spd dual-clutch auto	6-spd manual	7-spd dual-clutch auto
Length	4380mm	4052mm	4615mm
Width	1978mm	1802mm	1976mm
Height	1295mm	1153mm	1424mm
Wheelbase	2475mm	2370mm	2761mm
Fuel tank	64 litres	40 litres	63 litres
Range	497 miles	246 miles	328 miles
Boot	150 litres (f), 162 litres (r)	98 litres	430 litres
Front suspension	MacPherson struts, coil springs, anti-roll bar	Double wishbones, coil springs, anti-roll bar	MacPherson struts, coil springs, anti-roll bar
Rear suspension	MacPherson struts, coil springs, anti-roll bar	Double wishbones, coil springs, anti-roll bar	Multi-link, coil springs, anti-roll bar
Brakes	330mm ventilated discs (f), 299mm ventilated discs (r)	350mm ventilated discs (f), 332mm ventilated discs (r)	360mm ventilated discs (f), 350mm ventilated discs (r)
Wheels	8Jx20in (f), 9.5Jx20in (r)	7.5Jx17in (f), 9.5Jx18in (r)	8Jx18in (winter)
Tyres	235/40 ZR20 (f), 265/35 ZR20 (r)	205/45 ZR17 (f), 265/35 ZR18 (r)	235/40 ZR18 (winter)

GOALPOSTS: MOVED

Volkswagen's latest Golf may be a class act, but does it have the all-round appeal to beat the Audi A3, Ford Focus and Volvo V40? You bet it does, says **Nic Cackett**

PHOTOGRAPHY STAN PAPIOR

FORD FOCUS
The popular vote and the one that has traditionally attracted the keener drivers.

AUDI A3
The company car of choice in this sector. It's classy and executive-friendly.

VOLVO V40
Scandinavian cool and Volvo-grade safety mixed with a retuned Ford Focus chassis.

Family hatchbacks form the backbone of the retail market, and the Volkswagen Golf is the cervical vertebrae. So popular and widespread is the Golf's gospel that an affection for four wheels is hardly required to know and love it intimately. Its carefully fostered reputation for solidity, quality and reliability makes the model's status as a driveway-warmer par excellence almost a given.

But even the most casual buyer can't help but notice that the family hatch sector is now teeming with talent. With the Golf occupying a middle ground between premium and mainstream, we've hooked the best of both worlds to sit alongside it. The latest Audi A3, the Golf's three-door half-sister, is our current company car of choice and richly deserving of its upmarket image and executive-friendly renown. Its counterpoint is the Ford Focus, a perennial global contender for the title of best hatchback ever thanks to its dependability and handling acumen. Our wildcard is the Volvo V40. Pricey, practical and suave, it commands fresh attention – especially since we happened upon its ideal spec earlier this year.

The Volvo's secret formula turned out to be the softer Dynamic chassis (rather than the Sport version) and 17-inch wheels combined with the 1.6-litre petrol engine in 177bhp T4 guise.

The Volvo is not alone in requiring a careful juggle of its available components. To be at its best, the A3 must also be selected with its standard SE suspension, meaning that it comes with the entry-level 120bhp 1.4 TFSI motor by default. With the Focus, we've lined up our Zetec-trimmed long-term test car, which is ideal, because it comes with the 123bhp technical marvel that is the 1.0-litre turbocharged triple.

Not to be outdone, the Golf, in range-topping GT format, comes with the latest 138bhp 1.4 TSI engine, which is capable of turning from a lusty four-pot into a measly twin when its Active Cylinder Technology (ACT) deems it necessary. Adding untidy acronyms to model names is rarely advisable, but it has been suggested that the Mk7 could use all the distinguishing features it can get. Granted, from the outside, it hardly seems to qualify as a redesign, but in the metal it's a different story. Stare for several seconds and, like a magic-eye poster, the new car's etched, angular lines begin to make sense. The Mk6's meandering figure has been chipped and chivvied into a marginally swankier arrowhead.

The subtlety of the Golf's rendering succeeds where the A3 does not. Audi's hatchback has the forgettable good looks of a backing dancer; side by side, it never draws much focus from the VW Group's superstar. The Volvo can, thanks to its cheek-sucking flanks, but its appearance is more reliant on big wheels than the Golf. In their company, the Focus, with its previously →

VOLKSWAGEN GOLF
The evolutionary-led newcomer that has it all to prove and everything to lose.

'The subtlety of the Golf's rendering succeeds where the A3 does not'

Golf is well judged on material quality; big screen is excellent

A3 radiates an upmarket feel, even in this basic guise

Focus's cabin feels somewhat lacking among this company

Volvo provides a clean-looking and usable environment

← keen veneer hammered flat by the adoption of a US-friendly look and perched on 16-inch wheels, is the aesthetic sad sack of the four.

That theme continues inside. Not being built to satisfy upscale sensibilities (and hindered by a lowly trim) the Ford's chest-out dashboard and button-wearing chintz is a McDonald's kids' play area to its rivals' five-star hotel rooms. Robustness and respectable space are readily apparent, but understated elegance is missing. The Audi has the latter in dark, velvety swathes, but it can't replicate the roominess, although that's in part due to its three-door layout (the Sportback is longer).

The Golf's cabin is a Cezanne pear to Audi's inky Caravaggio. Its sibling may get the deluxe switchgear and higher-grade material, but VW has cut its cloth with inch-perfect judgement. The result is airy by day, cosy at night and suggestive of broad knee and elbow latitude (the car is 56mm longer and 13mm wider than its predecessor). As a blend of tasteful form and ergonomic function, it is about as compelling as it gets in a compact, workaday offering. Its pièce de résistance is the optional eight-inch colour touchscreen, mounted centre stage and furnished with possibly the slickest interface yet installed in a motor car.

Volvo, despite a loftier starting price, cannot compete with the Golf's internal harmony, yet it is a mature, well organised and utterly usable space to sit in. Clever work in the back can't liberate all the space on offer elsewhere, but the inboard seats accommodate big shoulders better than its exterior dimensions suggest and the adaptable instrument cluster feeds information to the driver with Technicolor perkiness. The V40 is refreshingly free of pretension.

Appropriately, perhaps, for a firm that stakes its reputation on safety and stability, the T4 is the heftiest car here, at 1380kg. Despite boasting the quickest 0-62mph time, at 7.7sec, it feels it, too. The V40 shares its underpinnings with the Focus, but Volvo's comprehensive retune replaces some of the vivaciousness with a more impassive, surefooted attitude. This doesn't preclude its driver from pushing on – the engine's 177lb ft of muscular flex from 1600rpm is willing enough – but progress is accurate rather than agile. Turn-in crispness is faintly dulled by the Dynamic suspension, but it's

an acceptable trade-off for better compliancy, and only the calibre of its rivals highlights the telltale shimmy of surface imperfections inside.

Driving the Ford for all of 90 seconds highlights this difference. In many ways, its renowned ride is a curious concoction and manifests as a springy, ground-hugging awareness of the wheels. The Focus has a way of moulding every surface into the same background encounter while you concentrate on steering through its pleasantly elasticised rack. The car is some 100kg lighter than the Volvo, and it shows, particularly over the front end, where its tiny engine liberates an already first-rate change of direction. Despite being the slowest model on test, the Ford rarely appears lead-footed or out of puff, largely by virtue of the triple's willingness to rev.

Credibly, it hardly seems any slower than the A3, even though it cedes a further 100kg and two full seconds in the 62mph sprint to the Audi. This may be because the A3's new 1.4-litre four-pot (shared with the Golf) doesn't improve on the Focus's overboost-granted 148lb ft of peak torque, and is rather flat towards its redline. That said, it's naturally more refined than the Ford's rasping triple and is almost as economical, returning a claimed 54.3mpg versus 56.5mpg on a combined cycle. Due to our care with the spec, the A3 rides with uncommon decorum for a car wearing the four rings, even on optional 17-inch wheels. Body control is tauter than with the Focus, and there is more grip in evidence, too. In fact, on a rain-soaked constant radius, its diligence at the front allows its rear end to be brought merrily into play. The result would be absorbing if the hatchback didn't hold its driver at Audi's habitual arm's length. The now-ubiquitous electric power steering means that no car here proffers genuine feedback, but the A3's wheel – hazily light just off centre, bulkily →

New Golf is longer and wider and all its occupants benefit

Focus serves up more rear space than the A3 or V40

Sportback (five-door) A3 will offer more room than this

V40's inboard rear seats liberate good shoulder room

'The Golf feels markedly quicker than its 8.4sec 0-62mph sprint suggests'

← contrived beyond – shrouds too much enthusiasm. It's all the more striking when you discover that the Golf does not submit to the same malaise. Befitting its ambience, it is a superbly well rounded steer. Our test car came with 10mm lower sports suspension and optional adaptive dampers, but this trimmed none of its finesse. It doesn't ride with Ford's organic sponginess but canters almost silently with unruffled and overt sophistication and barely feels like a hatchback at all. Refinement has been augmented, too. It is by some margin the quietest car on test here, and especially when tasked with a motorway journey.

Perhaps it is here that the Golf is most at home. Certainly, this is where the brawnier version of the same 1.4-litre engine takes every chance to imperceptibly deactivate two cylinders. The fuel-saving function helps it to class-leading efficiency (58.9mpg and 109g/km of CO_2 – 2g/km less than the smaller-engined Focus), but don't expect it to run on two cylinders all that often because even the faintest acceleration reverts to four-pot ignition. And with 184lb ft of torque available from 1500rpm, the Golf is conspicuously rapid. At 1270kg, it's far lighter than the V40, and it feels markedly quicker than its 8.4sec 0-62mph sprint suggests. The motor seems far more limber in this higher-output form and, mated to a confidence-inspiring, pliant chassis, the temptation is to extract its full potential at every opportunity.

Zealous driving tends to be what divides the exemplary generations of Golf from the also-rans, and the Mk7, with the same tenacious front end as the A3 but a less contrived steering feel, is remarkably well provisioned in that regard. Balance, steadiness and innate predictability are intrinsic, and it's noticeably more involving than the Volvo or Audi. At seven-tenths, it might even be more satisfying than the Focus. But push beyond that and the Ford's greater delicacy still does a better, more natural job of detailing what it's doing.

So, the result. There is no bottom-of-the-pile tag in this test. Simply making it on to the running order is a profound achievement, considering those that didn't. Finishing fourth is, therefore, no dishonour for the V40. Volvo's hatchback is the best model that the company makes and a tribute to its rediscovered enthusiasm for producing cars

The Golf and A3 share much but react differently

Same basic chassis but the Focus feels alert, V40 stable

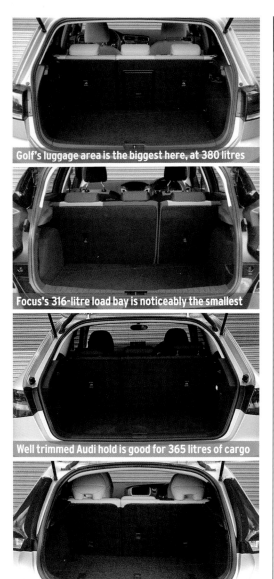

Golf's luggage area is the biggest here, at 380 litres

Focus's 316-litre load bay is noticeably the smallest

Well trimmed Audi hold is good for 365 litres of cargo

You can carry up to 335 litres in the Volvo's boot

	Volkswagen Golf 1.4 TSI GT 5dr	Ford Focus 1.0T Ecoboost Zetec 5dr	Audi A3 1.4 TFSI	Volvo V40 T4 SE Lux Nav
	1	**2**	**3**	**4**
VERDICT	The complete CV. Classy and more desirable than ever	Practical, clever and capable. Still offers the best value	A fine hatch and an even better buying bet; needs more soul	Volvo's finest. Overpriced perhaps, but a lot to like
RATING	★★★★½	★★★★☆	★★★★☆	★★★½☆
Price	£22,960	£17,745	£18,560	£26,930
0-62mph	8.4sec	11.3sec	9.3sec	7.3sec
Top speed	131mph	120mph	126mph	140mph
Economy	58.9mpg (combined)	56.5mpg (combined)	54.3mpg (combined)	51.4mpg (combined)
CO_2 emissions	109g/km	114g/km	120g/km	129g/km
Kerb weight	1270kg	1270kg	1175kg	1380kg
Engine layout	4 cyls in line, 1395cc, turbo, petrol	3 cyls in line, 999cc, turbo, petrol	4 cyls in line, 1395cc, turbo, petrol	4 cyl in line, 1596cc, turbo, petrol
Installation	Front, transverse, FWD	Front, transverse, FWD	Front, transverse, FWD	Front, transverse, FWD
Power	138bhp at 4500-6000rpm	123bhp at 6000rpm	120bhp at 5000-6000rpm	177bhp at 5700rpm
Torque	184lb ft at 1500-3500rpm	125lb ft (148lb ft on overboost) at 1500-4500rpm	148lb ft at 1400-4000rpm	177lb ft at 1600-5000rpm
Power to weight	108bhp per tonne	97bhp per tonne	102bhp per tonne	129bhp per tonne
Specific output	99bhp per litre	123bhp per litre	86bhp per litre	111bhp per litre
Compression ratio	10.5:1	12.0:1	10.5:1	10:1
Gearbox	6-spd manual	6-spd manual	6-spd manual	6-spd manual
Length	4255mm	4358mm	4237mm	4369mm
Width	1799mm	1858mm	1777mm	1802mm
Height	1452mm	1484mm	1421mm	1445mm
Wheelbase	2637mm	2648mm	2601mm	2647mm
Fuel tank	50 litres	55 litres	50 litres	62 litres
Range	665 miles	687 miles	601 miles	705 miles
Boot	380 litres	316 litres	365 litres	335 litres
Front suspension	MacPherson struts, coil springs, anti-roll bar	MacPherson struts, coil springs, anti-roll bar	MacPherson struts, coil springs, anti-roll bar	MacPherson struts, coil springs, anti-roll bar
Rear suspension	Multi-link, coil springs, anti-roll bar	Multi-link, coil springs, anti-roll bar	Multi-link, coil springs, anti-roll bar	Multi-link, coil springs, anti-roll bar
Brakes	288mm ventilated discs (f), 272mm discs (r)	278mm ventilated discs (f), 271mm discs (i)	381mm ventilated discs (f), 381mm discs (r)	300mm ventilated discs (f), 280mm discs (r)
Wheels	7Jx17in	7Jx16in	6.5Jx16in	7.0Jx17in
Tyres	225/45 R17	215/55 R16	205/55 R16	205/55 R17

infused with a distinctive character. Some testers considered it the best-looking machine on test, and no one suggested a foible without first expressing admiration for it. Tellingly, then, our biggest reservation is the asking price. Despite the extra power it affords, £26,930 before options for the admittedly high-spec T4 is simply too much.

Third and second are also divided by price, but overall the A3 and Focus sit practically on top of each other. The new A3 is a car of panache and high appeal. Ingratiatingly, it is at its best in base SE trim thanks to the pliancy of the standard suspension, and it offers surprisingly decent value for money considering the lavish fixtures and fittings within. Nevertheless, the A3 remains a somewhat sterile device and, in our eyes, the Ford edges ahead.

Shorn of its animated control surfaces and clever engine, the Focus would surely have taken a nosedive in this company. The cabin is a country mile behind its rivals', even allowing for the fact that this is the cheapest car here, at £17,945. But Ford's blue-collar protagonist remains a deserving hero. It may well be the Golf that has served as a benchmark for the public's wider automotive expectation over the past 40 years, but ever since 1998, when Ford dropped 'control blade' into our working lexicon, the Focus has shown that there is a practical, price-sensitive way of keeping driver pleasure at the forefront of the mainstream.

Volkswagen, meanwhile, has rarely risked revolution. Just as there are no substantial flaws with the latest Golf, so there are no spectacular steps forward, either. But the persuasiveness of slow evolution is undeniable. As a package, it's so convincingly accomplished that it's hard to acknowledge that you're not being treated to a superlative dynamic experience. ◳

Preaching ★★★ to the ★★★★ unconverted

Bentley's latest Continental GTC Speed is the world's fastest four-seat drop-top. **Andrew Frankel** heads to California to drive it

PHOTOGRAPHY STAN PAPIOR

eally, I should hate this car. Nine of them parked in a row outside the Mandarin Oriental in San Francisco in colours from gold to red strike an inadvertent pose that tells you much about how Bentley is viewed by the world. It is, at best, a gaudy start to our journey.

A conversation with this magazine's former chief sub-editor, one James May, comes into my head. Years ago he bought an old Bentley T2 because then they were so much cooler than their Rolls-Royce equivalents. But five years ago, when Bentley had become so successful that production overflowed from Crewe into a Volkswagen facility in Dresden, he sold it and bought an old Rolls. He liked Bentleys, but not their image.

But that's not why I should hate the GTC Speed. If you blamed cars for the people who drove them, there's many a marque that would be kicked from pillar to post on a weekly basis on these pages. No, the GTC is everything I don't want in an expensive, fast and sporting car. Which is to say it is both open and heavy. Bentley makes much of the fact that this is the fastest open four-seater in the world, with a claimed top speed of 202mph, thanks to the McLaren F1-teasing 616bhp boasted by its twin-turbo 6.0-litre engine. What it's less keen to publicise is that, thanks to a kerb weight just five kilos short of 2.5 tonnes, its power-to-weight ratio is inferior to that of a Porsche Cayman R.

And yet when I slide into the deep, sculpted chair, look around what remains one of the

The GTC Speed feels the need to pause before springing into action

★ ★ ★
★ ★ ★

Empty desert roads proved a temptation too hard to resist

← best-looking, best-finished interiors of any car at any price and hear the far-off thunder of those dozen pistons shuttling impatiently up and down their bores, I feel a wave of anticipation penetrating the brittle carapace of jet-lagged, jaundiced hack. I'm excited about this, and so I damned well should be.

For the next two days we're going to do little else but drive. Leaving town via the Golden Gate Bridge, the route takes us east past California's state capital, Sacramento, before heading up into the mountains to Lake Tahoe. From there we turn south and stay at altitudes twice the height of Ben Nevis all the way past Yosemite National Park to Mammoth Lakes before plunging down to the floor of the Mojave Desert. Here we'll find both Death Valley and Las Vegas, where I may fail to

resist the bombardment of opportunities to make cheap gags about having finally found the ideal environment in which to test a convertible Bentley.

We did have a plan to swing off the route to the El Mirage lake bed, a place unburdened by speed limits, and try to hit 200mph with the roof down (you may recall my futile attempts to do as much in the previous GTC Speed at Nardo, ending in utter frustration at 197mph), but one look at the winter-specification Dunlops Bentley had fitted put paid to that. The thought of the more-than interesting insurance claim resulting from that plan going wrong was all the incentive I needed to mothball that particular project for another day.

Now we should look more closely at what will be taking us on this substantial journey. The problem is we all think we know this car. It's a

GTC mechanically tweaked just enough to enable Bentley to make weapons-grade claims about its performance. This despite the power and speed records it has broken being held by its predecessor and it moving the game on by a fractional amount: 0.4sec off the 0-62mph time, a scant 2mph added to the top speed and all courtesy of a rise in engine power of a little more than two per cent.

In fact, there's more to this GTC than that. There are things you need to know about Bentley before you can understand a car like this. First, Bentley is always, and I do mean always, conservative in its claims. So if it says its engine has 616bhp, it means 616bhp in the hottest, thinnest air any owner is ever likely to find. Likewise, when it says the car will do 202mph, it touchingly elects not to mention that it'll also do 203, 204 and more. In another Nardo

Pan-California/Nevada odyssey took in iconic places and unlikely backwaters via interstates and mountain passes; you don't need a 616bhp W12 to enjoy the trip, but it helps

Technicolour line-up of GTC Speeds paints a gaudy picture of ostentatious excess, but taken in isolation — and on an inspiring drive — the Bentley's true qualities shine through

The GTC Speed is rapid but too heavy for true sports car status

jaunt with a Flying Spur years back, a car with a claimed top speed of 195mph was still accelerating at 208mph when it hit its rev limiter in top.

Less excitingly, but just as relevantly, Bentley has gone over the rest of the car to make sure it can cope with the power and performance available. Look at the small print and you will find revised spring rates, fatter anti-roll bars, a 10mm drop in ride height and new software for its Servotronic steering. Like its hard-topped GT Speed coupé brother, it now also enjoys the benefits of a new eight-speed gearbox, a worthwhile addition for all sorts of reasons, not least of which being that it extends the car's miserable range by 15 per cent.

Still, this is not a car die-hard sports car fans will find themselves instantly attracted to. Far heavier than the stockiest new Range Rover, it feels the need to pause before springing into action,

like an overweight man trying to emerge from an armchair in a hurry. For all its on-paper speed, you are aware of a certain *avoirdupois* that needs to be overcome. Only when speeds rise and inertia turns to momentum does it feel worthy of the mighty performance claims – including a sub-10.0sec 0-100mph capability – made on its behalf.

Soon enough there will be time to uncover more of this character trait, but for now we're schlepping east in heavy interstate traffic and I'm struck not so much by what it's doing as what it is not. It's not annoying me. I'm not wondering why the interior feels so cheap, as you might in a Porsche 911 Turbo cabriolet, or why a car as big as an Aston Martin DB9 Volante still has inadequate legroom for the driver. And unlike the Mercedes-Benz SL, it has a pair of small but viable rear seats.

Then the Bentley's true abilities begin to →

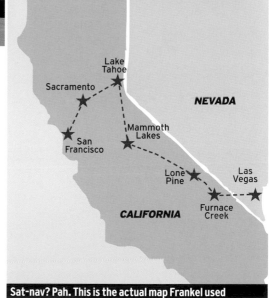

Sat-nav? Pah. This is the actual map Frankel used

★ ★

The Bentley is a rarity: a car that is better in practice than in theory

★ ★

The Bentley proved to be a blisteringly effective GT car

High-speed cruising was interrupted by scenic stops

Taste police wanted to check Frankel's licence to pose

← reveal themselves. First is the ride quality, which would be a triumph in a coupé, let alone a wobbly convertible. But the GTC Speed doesn't wobble, so its gait can be as soft as its structure is stiff. The wind management is so good that voices need never be raised and, as we discover up at 8000ft, the heating is so effective that you can drive it in temperatures well below zero without a coat.

Up in the mountains we find a road hard-packed in snow that has clearly been there for months yet upon which no vehicle has travelled. Admittedly more as an amusing displacement activity than a hard-nosed road testing imperative, I nevertheless feel obliged to discover what happens when you turn off all the electronics and attempt to deploy 616bhp on snow. It spins all four wheels for sure and produces a mighty roar but, on those trusty winter Dunlops, substantial thrust remains.

Even so, I can't help thinking that all those hundreds of miles of gentle cruising punctuated by occasional moments of light relief (usually characterised by discovering yet more cruel and

unusual ways of persuading the Bentley to break traction) is a mere prelude for what is to come.

The 25-mile drive from frozen Mammoth Lakes to the aptly titled Furnace Creek – the lowest, driest place in the US and officially the hottest place on earth – provides it. Here roads run so straight across such featureless moonscapes that state troopers have no chance of hiding, so they tend not to bother. So you up the pace, feeling the Bentley shed its sloth with every additional mile per hour. Nor do you have to worry about the poor and often violently undulating road surface, as the weight actually helps by bludgeoning the road

Hottest place on earth demanded a top-down breeze

The GTC Speed is remarkably agile and engaging for such a heavy car

	Bentley Continental GTC Speed	Aston Martin DB9 Volante
VERDICT	Heavy, but a fast, usable and magnificent beast	Fun to drive, well balanced and a great open-top GT
RATING	★★★★☆	★★★★☆
Price	£167,900	£141,995
0-60mph	4.1sec	4.6sec
Top speed	202mph	183mph
Economy	19.0mpg	18.2mpg
CO₂ emissions	347g/km	368g/km
Kerb weight	2495kg	1890kg
Engine layout	W12, 5594cc, twin-turbo, petrol	V12, 5935cc, petrol
Installation	Longitudinal, front, 4WD	Longitudinal, front, RWD
Power	616bhp at 6000rpm	510bhp at 6500rpm
Torque	590lb ft at 2000rpm	457lb ft at 5500rpm
Power to weight	247bhp per tonne	269bhp per tonne
Specific output	103bhp per litre	85bhp per litre
Compression ratio	9.0:1	10.9:1
Gearbox	8-spd automatic	6-spd automatic
Length	4906mm	4720mm
Width	1966mm	2061mm
Height	1393mm	1282mm
Wheelbase	2746mm	2740mm
Fuel tank	90 litres	78 litres
Range	320 miles	312 miles
Boot	230 litres	172 litres
Front suspension	Double wishbones, air springs, anti-roll bar	Double wishbones, coil springs, anti-roll bar
Rear suspension	Multi-link, air springs, anti-roll bar	Double wishbones, coil springs, anti-roll bar
Brakes	405mm ventilated discs (f), 335mm ventilated discs (r)	398mm carbon-ceramic discs (f), 360mm carbon-ceramic discs (r)
Wheels	9.5Jx21in	8.5Jx20in (f), 11Jx20in (r)
Tyres	275/35 ZR21	245/35 ZR20 (f), 295/30 ZR20 (r)

into submission. With the iron will conferred by its electronic dampers, you'll find the GTC has body control of which any car maker would be proud.

Back in the mountains and it surprises again. Bluntly, no 2.5-tonne convertible has any business handling as well as this. So long as the corner is quick enough, the GTC angles in accurately and eagerly, gripping hard and even offering some feel through its steering wheel. Ultimately there is understeer, but it is mild and, compared to the alternative, very welcome. If there's a problem, it is that you have to qualify its actions; it's certainly extraordinary, but only for such a heavy and structurally compromised car. The DB9 Volante, Ferrari California, Merc SL and 911 Turbo cabrio are all more nimble and rewarding to drive, and as the heaviest is well over half a tonne lighter than the GTC, it would be strange were it any other way.

But what it lacks in driver involvement, it recovers in areas less exciting to discuss but far more relevant to the real world in which rather more examples will live than the Utopian dreamland in which I've been operating these past few days. It proves convertibles don't have to be difficult to climb in and out of and that just because it's expensive and built in low volumes, its interior doesn't have to be an ergonomic mess. Nor do I see any reason to modify my view that it possesses the highest-quality, most refined fabric roof on sale.

Bentley was clever in launching the GTC Speed this way. Some cars get under your skin almost from the moment you see them; the GTC is the reverse and, as such, far more likely to get up your nose. You need hours and miles to see past its ostentatious appearance and headline-hungry stats to discover the real car beneath. Only then will you find that a machine you'd have dismissed as a charlatan Jack of all trades just days before turns out to be something completely different. No, it's not as pretty as a DB9, as dynamic as a California or, I expect, as explosively rapid as an SL63 AMG. But it is a class rarity: a car better in practice than theory, because it works in all seasons for most reasons. What appeared at first to be an unnecessarily ostentatious wealth statement turns out to be an entirely convincing, consummate all-rounder.

Turns out I didn't hate it all. In fact, I really rather liked it. A

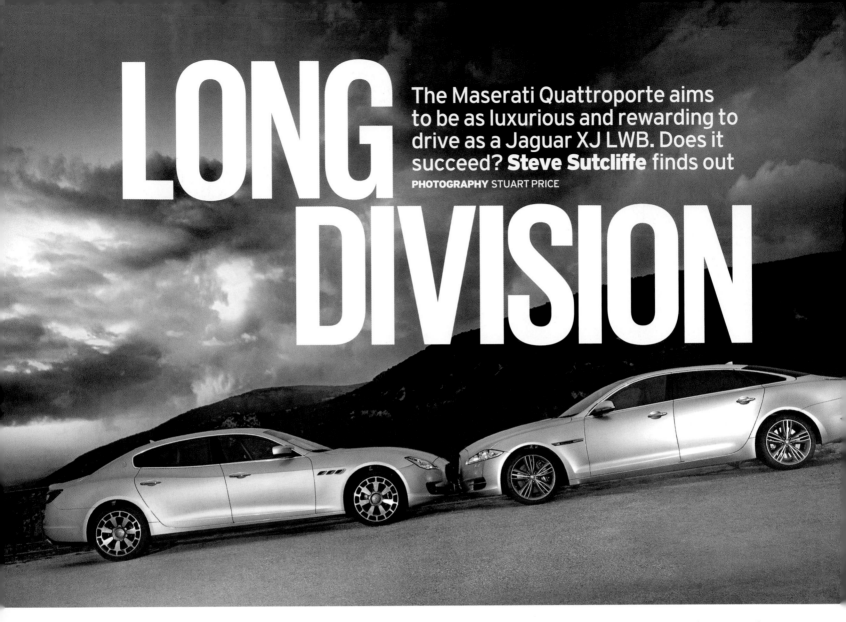

LONG DIVISION

The Maserati Quattroporte aims to be as luxurious and rewarding to drive as a Jaguar XJ LWB. Does it succeed? **Steve Sutcliffe** finds out

PHOTOGRAPHY STUART PRICE

One of the first assignments I was ever sent on by this magazine was to drive Maserati's then-brand-new one-make racing car, the Barchetta. The company has come a long way since then; since Ferrari became involved in 1997, Maserati has evolved gradually to a point where it now sells a steady 5000 to 6000 cars a year worldwide.

By 2015, though, the powers that be intend to increase that number tenfold, to a vaguely astonishing 50,000 cars a year. And the masterplan starts right here, with the all-new twin-turbo Quattroporte V8 whose underpinnings – indeed, whose entire engineering ethos – will provide the platform from which to march onward and upward.

It's an exciting car with which to enter an exciting new passage in history for what remains one of motoring's most iconic brands. Everyone loves a big Maser, after all, and they don't come much bigger than the 5262mm-long Quattroporte.

The vast length between the wheels is there to increase rear legroom by more than 100mm compared with the previous model, and this exists unashamedly to satisfy the Chinese market, which at the moment appears to be interested only in cars that have as much room in their rear chairs as you'll find in the Royal Albert Hall. Hence the reason why we've chosen to compare it with the long-wheelbase version of Jaguar's established class champion, the seductively styled, not to mention rather tasty to drive, XJ Supersport V8.

The similarities between these two leviathans are numerous and become clear from the moment they square up to one another. In the metal, they both appear genuinely enormous, occupying nigh-on 11 metres of road space when positioned nose to nose for our photograph (above).

As this story went to press, Maserati still had to confirm the price of the new Quattroporte, but it was expected to come in at "approximately £110,000". It's marginally less well equipped than the £95,235 Jaguar, whose options list is short only because Jaguar chooses to offer the car with just about everything in situ.

Drivers will feel bewildered at being able to summon

A good environment for the driver; more kit than in the Maser

The Quattroporte's front has the wow factor its rear lacks

Each of these cars is fearsomely quick in a straight line

Even in the hardware stakes, there's an unusual amount of common ground that's shared between the two of them. Both are powered by V8 engines and deploy their reserves via the same ZF eight-speed automatic gearbox with paddle shifters.

The Maserati blows through two turbochargers to help its 3.8-litre engine produce a thumping 523bhp at 6800rpm and 479lb ft of torque between 2000rpm and 4000rpm, with an overboost to 523lb ft available in bursts. The Jaguar, on the other hand, uses supercharging to encourage its 5.0-litre V8 to produce 503bhp at 6000rpm and 461lb ft between 2500rpm and 5500rpm.

The Jaguar is fractionally lighter, at 1955kg. It's also a touch more economical, with an official combined figure of 25.0mpg compared with 23.9mpg for the Quattroporte. Both have boots that are big enough to house a small family of servants for at least a weekend (Maserati 530 litres, Jag 520 litres) and both have more legroom on offer in their back seats than any ordinarily proportioned human could ever wish for.

There's one aspect that separates them wildly on the spec sheet, though: their relative top speeds. The Jag's is the standard-issue, limited-to-155mph staple that you'd expect. But the Maserati (being a Maserati) has no limiter whatsoever, which means that it will do 191mph flat out, thereby making it no less than... the fastest production saloon in the world.

Having said that, what's perhaps more revealing is that their 0-62mph claims are identical, at 4.7sec apiece. In the real world, in other words, they appear to be all but inseparable in a straight line, and that's precisely how it feels on the road.

They both feel outrageously fast, quite frankly, if and when you find a half-decent piece of road on which to let rip and there's no-one else around to become upset. I say this only because watching a two-tonne car that's this long, but also this rapid, come hurtling towards you on a single-carriageway road can, and often does, prove quite disturbing for other road users.

Of the two, the Maserati feels marginally more manic for pure acceleration, even if its turbocharged engine can't quite summon its torque in the same way that the Jag's quicker-responding supercharged V8 can.

But in neither instance is the driver going to feel short-changed by the level of basic performance that's on offer. In both cases, in fact, most drivers will feel quite bewildered at being able to summon Porsche 911-rivalling performance from cars as vast and potentially cumbersome as these.

Except, in reality, neither car throws its hands in the air and cries enough if you take it by the scruff and drive it hard. (I'm aware that these are limos and that they will rarely be driven to their limits, but Maserati still claims that the vast majority of Quattroporte owners want their cars to drive "sportily", and the mere name of the Jaguar would suggest that it is aimed towards the keener driver). In the Maserati, you can select a Sport function that stiffens the dampers and sharpens body control at a stroke. →

11-rivalling performance from cars as vast as these

THE VIDEOS OF THE YEAR

Which were the most popular videos on Autocar.co.uk in 2013? **Stuart Milne** has crunched the numbers to find out

WATCH

Lamborghini Aventador Roadster

This convertible version of one of the maddest and baddest supercars on the market can hit 217mph with the roof down. Steve Sutcliffe discovers if there's more to the latest drop-top Lambo than thundering straight-line thrills.

WATCH

World's fastest Minis go head-to-head

The Mini John Cooper Works GP is the fastest production Mini ever, according to BMW. That's all well and good, but we found what could be the quickest Mini ever, the Suzuki Hayabusa-engined ZCars Mini Busa. Cue fireworks...

WATCH

Audi R8 V10 Plus vs Ducati Diavel: 0-150-0mph

The Ducati Diavel superbike has twice the power-to-weight of the mighty Audi R8 V10 Plus, but which is quicker from a standstill to 150mph and back again? As our video shows, the result isn't as clear-cut as you'd think.

WATCH

Ultimate off-road drag race

Who can resist the lure of a damp, muddy field? Not Autocar's testers, who take to the grass to assess the off-road abilities of the latest Range Rover and supercar-rivalling Porsche Cayenne Turbo.

Geneva Motor Show round-up

The Geneva motor show was packed with highlights and included one of the most astonishing collections of brand spanking new supercars for many years. We take a look back at the first major European show of 2013.

Winter tyres vs 4x4 – snow tyre test

It was the argument of the winter: 4x4 or winter tyres? Andrew Frankel takes two Skoda Yetis - one front-wheel-drive on winter tyres, and the other a 4x4 variant on regular rubber - to determine which performs best in the snow.

Maserati Quattroporte vs Jaguar XJ

The latest Maserati Quattroporte is big news for the Italian marque. The car is kick-starting the firm's ambitions to increase sales ten-fold, so the stakes have never been higher. We pitch it against the long-wheelbase Jaguar XJ.

Supercars in the snow

What do you do when your best-laid plans to film a showdown with a couple of meaty Audis, a Bentley Continental GT Speed, a Jaguar XKR-S and a Porsche 911 Carrera 4S are scuppered by a snow storm? Drive them anyway, of course.

Porsche Cayman review

Our expert testers put the latest Porsche Cayman S to the test. With more power, more comfort, a better interior and improved looks, can it really be capable of providing even more entertainment than the car it replaces?

Range Rover vs Porsche Cayenne tested on-road

We didn't just drive them on grass (see left). The all-new Range Rover is one of the best cars of the year, but can it hold a candle to the superb German engineering that underpins the mighty Cayenne? Steve Sutcliffe finds out.

FROM £500

FROM £895

Bangernomics
MANIFESTO

Bangernomics is all about saving money by buying and running the best used cars for the lowest outlay. **James Ruppert** explains how it's done

Bangernomics contrasts the absurd expense of buying a new car with the supreme good sense of buying a well used one. At a stroke, depreciation no longer becomes an issue, running costs are slashed and there are no finance charges to be endured.

Bangernomics makes you feel good about owning a car. In fact, you will have a warm, greenish glow from recycling a used car, prolonging its life and hopefully seeing a slightly larger bulge in your bank balance. Not only is Bangernomics easy, but it is also mostly fun. You learn some skills, waste less money and have a new topic of dinner party conversation.

So why buy a posh car just to drive a few miles to the train station each day? Why worry about leaving your pride and joy overnight in an urban street? Please allow me to explain.

1 WHY YOU SHOULD BE A STUDENT OF BANGERNOMICS

Buying and owning an older used car makes so much sense. For a start, it will save you money. Before a new car has turned a wheel, you can write off VAT, plus the dealer's charge to put it on the road, but the bad news doesn't end there. Depreciation takes an unhealthy bite out of the car's value, too.

2 BANGERNOMICS IS A STATE OF MIND

It is actually a different mental approach to motoring. You will own a car that is unlikely to drop in value much and it will be cheap to run. You won't be paying through the nose for

comprehensive insurance and you won't worry if it gets left overnight in a dodgy car park, or it gets scraped or dented. You won't care what the Joneses are driving because image is less important than practicality. Then, if you get bored with the banger or it breaks down and costs too much to fix, you simply get rid of it and your losses are minimal.

3 BANGERNOMICS DOESN'T MEAN THAT YOU'LL DRIVE A SHED

Used cars have never been cheaper. In the past few years, the fall in new car prices, cheap finance and a culture of increasingly rapid automotive obsolescence have meant that cars past their fifth birthday have never been as affordable as they are now. There are BMWs, Mercedes-Benzes and Audis out there that are great value.

4 THE BANGER DEFINED

To some people, it could be a 15-year-old hatchback with steel wheels and faded paintwork. However, the bottom Bangernomics line should always be that a banger must be any used car that you can afford to buy and run on your budget, without taking out a loan; you own it outright and live within your automotive means.

5 BANGERNOMICS MEANS THAT YOU CAN MOVE ON

There comes a point when a car is uneconomic to repair, so you simply buy another. Without worrying about finance payments or depreciation, you can sell the car for spares, or drive it to a salvage yard and start again. The trick is, of course, spotting when your banger is becoming a liability.

6 BANGERNOMICS IS GREEN

Bangernomics is recycling. The amount of natural resources and energy used in building a new car is phenomenal, so prolonging the life of a used car (and disposing of it responsibly) is a very green way to go motoring.

7 BANGERNOMICS ISN'T FOR EVERYONE

Anyone who is image conscious and spends most of Sunday with a bucket, sponge and polish might baulk at the ethics of Bangernomics. As might motoring snobs who must have the latest registration plate and model of car.

8 BANGERNOMICS IS FOR MOTORING ENTHUSIASTS

No, really. Although the money you save could be spent on lots of other things, like new kitchens and holidays, if you acquire a Bangernomic car as your daily driver, you could also buy that sports car you always promised yourself for some weekend fun. →

FROM £895

/ˈbænə(r)ˈnɒmɪks/

You will own a car that will not drop in value much and will be cheap to run

56 GYY

SMOKING HOT

It's all very well banging on about Bangernomics, but which cars make the best budget buys? Which well used models won't let you down? Clearly, some cars can take the punishment better than others. Here are my top five picks across different categories, and some hints about what to look out for when you're checking over your potential cut-price purchase.

TOP 5 TINY TOTS

The trouble with small cars is that they wear out more quickly. Whether it's their tiny engines, small wheels or slipping clutches, a hard-used tot can be a liability. All those stop-start journeys and car park dings mean that it's important to pick the right one.

FROM £299

NISSAN MICRA

Toy town styling, but town centre assault vehicle ability. The Micra is nippy enough with a good range of small and eager petrol and diesel engines that return from just under 50mpg to more than 60mpg. Not only that, but it is also surprisingly quiet on the motorway. The driver gets lots of space and an excellent driving position, while all-round vision is great and the controls fall easily to hand. It's an old learner's favourite, though, which means clutches might have taken abuse. Batteries drained quickly on early examples, and watch out for smoke on the diesels – a sign that the turbo bearings are failing.

BANGERS

FROM £400

DAIHATSU CUORE

The Cuore is rare, weighs nowt, costs less than nowt to run and the engine will buzz forever. Inside, it's bright, tight and cheap, but the drive is fine if you stick to urban roads, because there's enough power for town use and the compact dimensions make it easy to exploit gaps in traffic. The Cuore runs rings around those big, silly 4x4s that everyone else has because it's light and nimble. Some parts are hard to find, though. Look for rot and worn-out bits and bobs, from minor consumables to brakes and exhausts. Other than that, it will run and run.

FROM £399

DAEWOO MATIZ

Bug-eyed, pocket-size people carrier with a tight turning circle, which, combined with light power steering, means that manoeuvring is never a problem. The engines are eager and it's nippy where it matters, too. It's a tiny car but rides reasonably well and there's an almost sporty roar to the three-cylinder engine. Running costs are low, it will return 45mpg and the insurance group will be in single figures. The big service comes at 40,000 miles. Watch out for dents, bald tyres and badly worn upholstery.

FROM £250

FORD FIESTA

The Ford Ka might be the obvious choice, but the Fiesta is a tad more practical and just as much of an amusing device to drive. Throw it into a corner and it will bring you safely out the other side, but more importantly, replacement parts are plentiful, cheap and available at your local salvage yard if something breaks. The 1.3-litre engine is painfully slow, but cars equipped with it are among the cheapest to run when it comes to servicing and insurance. Avoid diesels and automatic transmissions and you shouldn't have a problem. Look out for rust, bald tyres, blowing exhausts and fading brakes.

FROM £200

VAUXHALL CORSA

Its Corsa by name and coarse by nature, but never mind that; Vauxhall's practical supermini is easy and cheap to buy, and that's the defining reason to buy Danger nomically. Low insurance, reasonable servicing costs, cheap parts and good fuel consumption are the plus points. If your expectations aren't too high in terms of specification or image, it has to be a Corsa, especially for first-time drivers. The teeny tiniest petrols, provided they are not worn out, can deliver up to 50mpg, while worn clutches, shot brakes and shabby, rusty bodies are the issues. Only buy with a full MOT for peace of mind.

TOP 5 BARGES

The great thing about these big old smokers is that no one wants them, what with their marginal fuel consumption, sky-high parts prices and long list of luxury features just waiting to go wrong. But if you don't do many miles and you need the cabin space, they could make sense for a discerning student of Bangernomics. Barges give you everything for nothing, but which are the ones to look out for?

FROM £895

MERCEDES-BENZ S-CLASS

We must travel back in time to the 1990s for our first taste of affordable luxury. The S-class is an old-school, slab-sided plutocrat's kind of Mercedes, and none the worse for that. Refinement levels are very high and comfort is not at issue. This is a quiet and sophisticated large car that's hard to fault. Often the bigger the engine, the cheaper they are, but whether you'd want to take on a full-house V12 is another matter. Six cylinders are fine, but at the Bangernomics end of the scale it's the small things that add up, so tyres, exhausts and brakes are where the expense can start.

FROM £395

FROM £495

FROM £695

HONDA LEGEND

In essence it's just a great big Accord, but look at it as a Lexus lite. The Honda utterly lacks any semblance of prestige despite its bulk, but that helps to keep prices on the floor. Every contemporary extra will be standard, so although it won't make you feel special on the outside, inside you really will have the last laugh as you fiddle with the ultra-reliable fixtures and fittings. In 1999 an upgraded model brought extra airbags, quieter engines and uprated brakes and suspension. Be wary if the ABS light comes on, and low oil pressure can be an issue. You really need to find one with a thorough service history.

LEXUS GS

Lots of standard equipment, sky-high build quality and brilliant engines. The GS can be expensive to own and it doesn't look or feel special enough against something like a BMW 5-series, but it easily beats one for kit. The GS is getting on a bit, but it remains fabulous value for money and can be bought with a high mileage without any worries. You just have to look at the consumables. Brakes, suspension and steering can all be quite tired by now. Also steer clear of any 'blinged' ones, which can be marginal and may never have been serviced by the previous owner.

VAUXHALL OMEGA

Imposing rear-drive saloons can be bought with all sorts of posh badges on them, but we think the traffic cops had it right with those big, white Senators and Omegas fitted with the blues and twos. It's a hefty old barge but a forgiving one. It always feels safe, too, and in top Elite trim an Omega is very comfy. The estate is massively practical, too. The Omega is starting to get old and some will be neglected, so choose carefully as shabby ones will cost money. Tyres, suspension, brakes and now rust are issues that can cause MOT failure, so get the old girl checked over thoroughly before committing to buy.

TOP 5 UGLY CARS

Five cars that may be ugly but do their jobs beautifully

FIAT DOBLO FROM £495

Almost beaten to death with an ugly stick, but the Doblo still has charm, at least for a people carrier that's based on a working van. It's also painfully slow, but nothing else can pack people and luggage into such a confined – and aesthetically challenged – space.

FIAT MULTIPLA FROM £400

Another apparently wilfully ugly Fiat, but inside you'll discover that sitting three abreast front and back makes perfect sense. The boot is also a decent size and, best of all, it's short, so it's a doddle to park. How beautiful is that?

FORD SCORPIO FROM £695

Clearly styled like a guppy, but this is no fish out of water. Ford's big executive saloon has everything you need. Running costs are low, equipment lists are high and prices are marginal. Great value if you want a comfy large car for towing or just cruising.

DAIHATSU GRAND MOVE FROM £595

It's a tiny box on wheels, but the trick is that all the seats fold flat into a double bed. That's right, it's huge inside, and tall enough for everyone to wear a top hat. So why stick with a small, good-looking hatch with no interior space when you could have one of these?

HYUNDAI COUPE FROM £500

For two years, from 2000 to 2002, the Coupé got a hideous four-eyed restyle, but underneath there are utterly reliable Hyundai mechanicals and a decent handling package. It's good value and manages to turn heads, as all good coupés should.

FROM £595

JAGUAR XJ8

Anything with a Jaguar badge is a quintessential Bangernomics barge, making an XJ8 probably one of the finest luxury cars that not much money will buy. Driving one will make you feel special and a bit regal, with an Edwardian interior combined with a responsive and silky V8 engine. The 3.2-litre is the entry-level model but doesn't feel it, and many owners report that they can coax 30mpg out of theirs. The Sovereign model is slightly bigger and addresses the issues of those who say that the previous iteration was too cramped inside. Common faults include electrical issues with the computer and warning lights, leaky air conditioning and squeaking auxiliary belts.

TOP 5 PAUPER'S PERFORMANCE CARS

Who said Bangernomics had to be boring? Why shouldn't a cheap car be either a quick one, or one that is fun to own, look at and drive? Performance fashions change rapidly, and those that get left behind become depreciated yet desirable vehicles.

FORD PUMA

Is there anything wrong with the perfectly formed Puma? These things are now criminally cheap. For some, those big arches aren't as full of rubber as they should be, and what's the point of the 1.6 when the 1.7 is so much better? The 1.4, meanwhile, manages the impossible by making the Puma seem almost sluggish. It's a Fiesta underneath, and that's a good thing. Engines go on forever, but the suspension may need fettling, so consider new shocks and rubbers. It gets through brakes quickly, and look out for MOT-failure rust.

FROM £395

HYUNDAI COUPE

For those who missed the Ford Capri, here is the equivalent for the 1990s and 2000s. Hyundai's Coupé succeeded in its efforts to look like a much hotter and more expensive sports car. It was never a hardcore racer, but it clings on to corners enthusiastically enough, provided you don't push too hard. Stick to the 2.0-litre engine for economy and insurance purposes. It has just about enough go, too, but it's the V6 that suits the car best and can be among the cheapest buys. Korean-tough mechanicals don't cause problems, but minor electrical glitches do, such as dicky remote central locking and sticky sunroofs.

FROM £1000

SEAT LEON

It's hard not to like, or indeed love, the Seat Leon, and all the more so if it comes in a distinctly parrot-coloured hue. Here's a family hatchback with a decent turn of speed when found in 1.8 Cupra trim. It's devoid of Volkswagen's premium pricing, so the Leon is the best-value GTI that any of us can buy. While the sensible money would seek out an oil-burner, the free spirit will be happy with the purposeful Cupra. The biggest worry is the turbo; you won't want that to let go in a cloud of smoke.

FROM £800

VOLVO 850 T-5R

This is a truly evil and very naughty Volvo indeed. Image-wise, the T-5R took the marque from green wellies to loads of welly in about the same time as it takes to get to 60mph (around 7.0sec). Step on the accelerator and the 2.3-litre five-pot barely hesitates. There's a distinctive, pleasing burble as the engine brings itself to the boil, then the turbo joins in to tug the big estate along with deceptive ease. Leaky rear main oil seal costs 50p on its own but £1000 to sort out. Air-con can go on the blink in an expensive way.

FROM £450

HONDA ACCORD COUPE

Often overlooked because no one knew it ever existed, here is the slightly interesting Accord with fewer doors and a sloping roof. Being a Honda, it is superbly built and very tough, and most on sale are tidy and have been well looked after by some old fella. There is an adequate 2.0-litre option, but the 3.0 V6 is rather more interesting and brings with it the extra specification. This is no perky little Prelude, and it should be in better nick than one of those. Look for worn brakes, some minor rust and possibly suspension bushes and shock absorbers.

FROM £500

Autocar Yearbook 2014

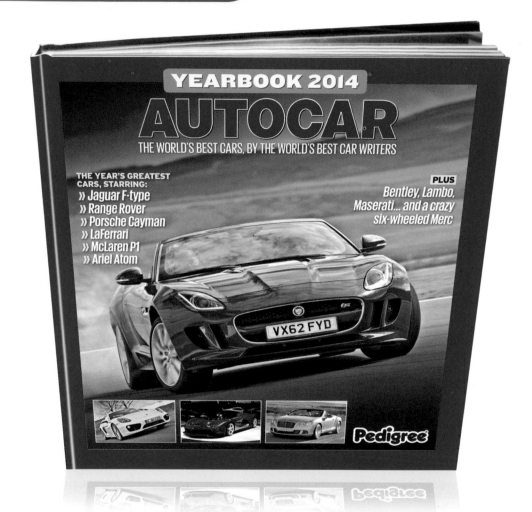

Visit **Pedigreebooks.com** to find out more on this year's **Autocar** Yearbook, scan with your mobile device to learn more.

Visit www.pedigreebooks.com

Pedigree Books, Beech Hill House, Walnut Gardens, Exeter EX4 4DH